SACROSANCTUM CONCILIUM
AND THE REFORM
OF THE LITURGY

SACROSANCTUM CONCILIUM

AND THE REFORM OF THE LITURGY

Proceedings from the 29th Annual Convention
of the Fellowship of Catholic Scholars

Kansas City, Missouri
September 22-24, 2006

Kenneth D. Whitehead, Editor

**Library of Congress
Cataloging-in-Publication Data**

(Has been applied for but is not available at time of publication.)

Distribution:

UNIVERSITY OF SCRANTON PRESS
Chicago Distribution Center
11030 S. Langley
Chicago, IL 60628

PRINTED IN THE UNITED STATES OF AMERICA

CONTENTS

Session V: Ecclesia de Eucharistia – Liturgy and Mission

Cardinal Wright Award Banquet

Holy Mass

INTRODUCTION TO THE CONVENTION PROGRAM

James and Helen Hull Hitchcock

"The Church draws her life from the Eucharist. This truth does not simply express a daily experience of faith, but recapitulates the heart of the mystery of the Church." Pope John Paul II wrote this at the beginning of his 14th and last encyclical, *Ecclesia de Eucharistia.* This great encyclical of the late pope on the subject of the Eucharist and its relationship to the Church appeared on Holy Thursday, 2003, nearly forty years after the Constitution on the Sacred Liturgy, *Sacrosanctum Concilium,* was promulgated by Pope Paul VI on December 4, 1963.

This year, at its 29th annual convention, the Fellowship of Catholic Scholars concludes its observance of the 40th anniversary of the end of the Second Vatican Council with an exploration of *Sacrosanctum Concilium* and some of the other documents of the Holy See on the liturgy issued since the Council. At our 28th annual convention last year, we focused upon the other acts and documents of Vatican II besides *Sacrosanctum Concilium* (covered in the volume *After Forty Years*). This year the very large subject of the reform of the liturgy mandated by Vatican II seemed to merit fully a program by itself.

The presentations printed here focus on several key aspects of the liturgy and its authentic reform and renewal from the perspective of the past four decades: Sacred Music; Art and Architecture; Scripture and Liturgical Translation; and the relation of the liturgy to the mission of the Church in our day—bearing in mind the words of the Council Fathers at the beginning of *Sacrosanctum Concilium:*

> While the Liturgy daily builds up those who are within into a Holy Temple of the Lord, into a dwelling place for God in the Spirit, to the mature measure of the fullness of Christ, at the same time it

marvelously strengthens their power to preach Christ, and thus shows forth the Church to those who are outside as a sign lifted up among the nations under which the scattered children of God may be gathered together, until there is one sheepfold and one shepherd (SC 2).

As Catholic scholars representing many academic disciplines, we have tried to take to heart the Council's words:

…the liturgy is the summit towards which the activity of the Church is directed; at the same time it is the font from which all her power flows. For the aim and object of apostolic works is that all who are made sons of God by faith and baptism should come together to praise God in the midst of His Church, to take part in the Sacrifice, and to eat the Lord's Supper.

The liturgy in its turn moves the faithful, filled with "the Paschal Sacraments," to be "one in holiness"; it prays that "they may hold fast in their lives to what they have grasped by their faith"; the renewal in the Eucharist of the covenant between the Lord and man draws the faithful into the compelling love of Christ and sets them on fire. From the Liturgy, therefore, especially from the Eucharist, as from a font, grace is poured forth upon us; and the sanctification of men in Christ and the glorification of God, to which all other activities of the Church are directed as toward their end, is achieved in the most efficacious possible way (SC 9, 10).

May we, through study and reflection, in worship and praise, be brought to a renewed understanding of this "font of grace," and recognize our privilege and duty to "show forth the Church" to others—to the greater glory of God.

I.

KEYNOTE ADDRESS

Sacrosanctum Concilium and The Recovery of the Sacred: Liturgy and Ritual

James Hitchcock

Liturgical change after the Second Vatican Council was guided by "experts" who implemented it through bureaucratic processes, but, despite the fact that most of those experts were highly educated in matters liturgical, for some reason they ignored the way in which the ritual of the Church is deeply and organically rooted in the mystical community and this ignorance severely damaged liturgical life in ways that are only now being seriously addressed.[1]

The Liturgical Movement underwent a radical change immediately after the Council, no longer aiming to lead worshippers ever more deeply into the divine mysteries but seeking instead to make liturgy "relevant" by minimizing its mystical elements and assimilating it to a community celebration. While there was some resistance on the part of a confused laity, this bureaucratic program largely succeeded, both because it was imposed, and because it actually did capture the spirit of the age, offering a liturgy that fit well with a relaxed suburban life style.

The familiar jibe that the difference between a terrorist and a liturgist is that it is possible to negotiate with a terrorist is in fact borne out in the history of the Liturgical Movement at its moment of victory, when Father Frederick McManus, soon to become the key liturgical bureaucrat in America, warned against compromise and misplaced solicitude for the concerns of people in the pews.[2] Another prominent priest-liturgist compared his task to that of a health officer sent to ignorant natives in the tropics. To those who resisted his ministrations he had one stern reminder: "It's the Law!"[3] A layman told a liturgical gathering that existing parishes were "at best harmless rest camps" for people who were incapable of understanding the Gospel, and he thought that "social scientists….would see them in pathological terms."[4]

One of the great unexplained ironies of recent Church history is how a Council that purportedly promised greater freedom to Catholics ended up, with regard to liturgy, setting in motion an iron-fisted authoritarianism that continues to the present day. Apparently the sources do not exist for a detailed history of how the Council's sparse words about the vernacular, much less its complete silence about the position of altars, within a short time were turned into universal laws enforced with often draconian severity by people who themselves ignored or defied those of higher authority than themselves.

A further irony still is the fact that lay resistance to liturgical change now often justifies itself by a rejection of clerical authority that was itself an unintended fruit of the Council. Concerning liturgy, many lay people understand that some of those in authority make unsupportable claims and that somehow they must find their own way.

Many traditional Catholics did indeed approach the liturgy as spectators, or as only marginal participants, and liturgical innovators correctly understood that liturgy is in some ways an expression of the life of the worshipping community. But the innovators had a radically impoverished, essentially secular, idea of what that expression might be, reducing "participation" merely to such things as singing and praying aloud and reducing "community" merely to those people actually gathered for worship at a particular moment, no longer with any sense of membership in the invisible and eternal Communion of Saints, of the Mystical Body.

A new puritanical spirit systematically, even fanatically, changed or discarded the architecture, symbolism, and music that spoke of eternity and transcendence and, as the poverty of this new spirit came belatedly to be recognized, sought to create new symbols (dancing, banners) by fiat, not comprehending the way in which genuine ritual has to be deeply embedded in the life of a community over a period of generations.[5]

This puritanism rested in part on the assumption that modernity is entirely pragmatic, that old things no longer speak to "modern man." But in their eagerness to be relevant, their determination to purge the liturgy of all its "magical" elements, liturgists drastically misread the direction of the culture, since pragmatic utilitarianism inevitably called forth its seeming opposite, so that such things as astrology, the occult, and even witchcraft suddenly achieved a new respectability, as the moralistic focus on "social problems" gave way to a "counter-culture" that castigated modern man precisely for his pragmatic philistinism. Discarded ritual elements like candles, incense, vestments, and chanting were resuscitated, but in an entirely new context—as servants of a compulsive search for ever more esoteric pleasures, ultimately those of the psychedelic "high." (One priest actually proposed "ritual drunkenness" as an appropriate element of liturgy.)[6] But such counterfeit ritual looks into the depths of the human psyche, never towards the eternal God, and is in some ways even more inimical to genuine religion than is sheer unbelief.[7]

The spiritual and psychological affects of all this went so deep that even now they are only imperfectly understood, often reduced merely to the level of personal preference. But uncontrolled liturgical change in effect pitted the liturgy against itself, setting up conflicts that remain unresolved. Liturgists seemed to have no understanding of the deep psychic disturbances caused by sudden, often radical, alterations in ritual life and in fact even lost sight of the elementary reality that liturgy *is* ritual—symbolic action occurring in sacred time and space,[8] heightened sensitivity to symbolic action, an economical condensation of a whole range of symbols.[9]

Church leaders on the whole failed to understand this because traditional Scholastic theology and Enlightenment rationalism alike made it difficult for them to comprehend adequately the nature of ritual and symbolic action, something that the study of the phenomenology of ritual might have provided.[10]

As Mary Douglas, the most astute critic of liturgical change, pointed out: "If a people takes a symbol that was originally meant for something else, and energetically holds on to that subverted symbol, its meaning for their personal life must be very profound."[11] In the words of Robert Redfield: "Men cease to believe because they cease to understand, and they cease to understand because they cease to do the things that express the understandings."[12]

Catholicism has always been rich in ritual gestures and symbols, but after the Council the renewed spirit of puritanism discarded many of those enduring symbols as "meaningless." In keeping with the rationalist mentality of the reformers, most liturgical change took place only on the conscious level, leading to what might be called the fallacy of explicitness—the meaning of the rituals was didactically explained in such a way as to render the symbols themselves superfluous.

At first the errors caused by this insensitivity were probably not intended. But as it became obvious to what degree change had disoriented the community, many innovators embraced disorientation as a positive good, because it "liberated" Catholics from what was now declared to be an oppressive and burdensome past.[13] The "purification" of worship, instead of opening ever deeper wellsprings of spirituality, often created a vacuum that was quickly filled by invasions from the secular culture.[14]

Sacred ritual always presents itself as divinely ordained,[15] but the speed with which liturgical changes were introduced, the confusing and often contradictory things said about them, the way in which they were decreed by committees and bureaucratic offices, the continuing debates, the replacement of sacred liturgical books by discardable leaflets, the wholesale destruction of so much that was venerable, and the endless tinkering—all this had the cumulative effect of making the liturgy seem an all-too-human activity, not a divine action, in which humans were privileged to participate but in something that they themselves had created.[16]

The very concept of "experimental" liturgy is destructive, implying as it does that the participants consciously manipulate it for their own purposes, then study the results in a clinical spirit. (Few of these "experiments" have ever been declared failures, even when the patient has been killed in the process.) Pope Benedict XVI has pointed out that the very idea of "creative" liturgy is fallacious, in that it treats liturgy as a human construct.[17]

Those who have experienced this at the deepest level are perhaps those who line up on opposite sides in the continuing liturgical wars. While most of the laity seem to accept passively whatever changes appear to be mandated, "traditionalists" believe that meaning can be recovered only by a return to the "old Mass," while liberals also seem to concede that the official rite is now barren and consequently assert an imperative to engage in continuing and ever more radical experimentation, both groups understanding that something profound has occurred.

Two categories of Catholics were especially affected by the post-conciliar liturgical crisis—impressionable young people and priests, whose identities were intimately bound up with the liturgy, experienced the chaos of the Church's ritual and organizational life. Adolescents in those years gained little experiential sense of a coherent and binding Catholicism, and many still have not. Although many experimental liturgies were crafted to attract young people, their chief effect was often to confirm the young in their alienation from the main body of the Church, while on the other side there was a profound clerical crisis, as the sacramental vocation itself was called into question. The apparent unraveling of priestly and religious life probably had far more to do with the weakening of the beliefs of ordinary Catholics than did direct attacks on those beliefs by dissident theologians.

When traditional liturgy was declared to be "meaningless," the engineers of change in reality often meant that it was meaningful in the wrong way—too "supernatural," too "vertical," too "archaic"— and they aimed to use liturgical change to bring about a change of attitude. For example, one general secretary of the International Committee for English in the Liturgy (ICEL) admitted that the reception of communion in the hand diminished a sense of reverence and quipped with apparent satisfaction that "the communion has become a cheap commodity, cheaper than pizza, because you have to pay for pizza."[18]

For awhile, in accordance with the traditional understanding of sacramental validity, liturgical changes, even of a fairly radical kind, were said not to affect the underlying truth of the Mass itself, so that virtually nothing a priest might do could affect the sacramental reality, so long as he correctly pronounced the words of institution. But it soon became obvious that it is not possible to separate liturgical issues from doctrine. The principle, *"Lex orandi est lex* credendi," recognizes that changes in the mode of worship can affect belief, and it is obvious that Catholics no longer all share the same theology of the Eucharist. Contrary to the facile explanations sometimes offered, radical liturgical change is not, and cannot be, merely a matter of the same beliefs expressed in new ways. The aversion that some Catholics have towards traditional liturgy, and their embrace of increasingly experimental forms, arise precisely from religious doubt, from a desire to reduce religion merely to some kind of spiritual searching.

One of the purposes of official ritual is to preserve the beliefs of the worshipping community during times when there is a danger of losing sight of those beliefs, to keep them intact until such times as they are rediscovered.[19] Thus, a concomitant danger in unauthorized liturgies is that the principle, *"Lex orandi est lex credendi,"* can be cited to prove that omissions, such as that of the Creed itself, reveal that such particular doctrines are no longer the teachings of the Church. Among practicing Catholics, it appears that even the concept of God is now weak and confused, encompassing everything from Chalcedonian orthodoxy through deism to a kind of self-deifying pantheism.

Obviously worshippers should be educated, as far as they are able, as to the meaning of the liturgy, and should be attentive to the action and should join in the prayers. But the degree to which there was already "participation" prior to the Council has been greatly underestimated. If nothing else, worshippers understood that something of eternal significance was taking place on the altar—that Christ Himself was present—and they assisted in a spirit of reverence. Ritual, in order to be authentic, does not require participants to have an emotional experience; often they participate in what may appear to be a routine spirit.[20] Most Catholics before the Council valued liturgical symbols highly, even when they did not fully comprehend their specific meanings.

But after the Council, as the inevitable result of insensitivity to the nature of ritual action, "meaningful" worship came to be defined by the congregation's own subjective experiences and only spontaneous worship could be genuine, an assumption that seemed finally to require that the congregation create its own liturgies. But, as Thomas Merton had warned:

> Secular personalism is a kind of craze for individuality, a rage for self-manifestation in which the highest value is the *recognition* of one's own uniqueness...On the contrary, Christian personalism does not require that the inmost secrets of our being be made manifest or public at all...what is manifested, proclaimed, celebrated and consummated in the liturgy is not my personality or yours but the personality of Christ the Lord...We sing alike, we pray alike, we adopt the same attitudes. Yet oddly this "sameness" does not wound our individuality.[21]

Classical ritual theory recognizes that the rites are not an expression of the mundane but are something that stands outside time; they are situations where man is stripped of everything ordinary and made aware of the powers that sustain the universe.[22] The rites embody personal commitments that transcend passing moods, embodying the participants' deepest understanding of the universe,[23] something that, paradoxically, eventually makes such ritual far more "relevant" than the kinds of observances that consciously seek that goal.

Virtually from the beginning, the Catholic Church, like some other great religions, tolerated and even encouraged a folk piety alongside its official worship, a piety that sustained the faithful in their personal lives. While the Mass itself was celebrated quite formally, in accordance with the often-praised spirit of Roman restraint, personal and subjective piety was expressed through private devotions.

But by suppressing those devotions, and attempting, at least for a time, to make the Eucharist virtually the only legitimate form of Catholic piety, the innovators created an emotional hunger that they then inappropriately tried to satisfy through the liturgy itself. The supreme irony of the Liturgical Movement was that it struggled for decades to make Catholics appreciate the Eucharist as the center of their lives but, once it had achieved its stated goals, participation in the Eucharist fell off sharply in almost all communities, one of the principal causes being the war on popular piety waged in the name of the liturgy. Popular devotions had sustained many Catholics in their faith in a personal way, so that, as they were pruned away to allow the Eucharist to stand out in all its glory, regard for the Mass itself declined.[24] (The Charismatic Movement then emerged as a new kind of expressive personal piety, but one that had few if any precedents in Catholic tradition.)

The present liturgical conflict is often presented as between "traditionalists" and "innovators," something that does not, however, pose the issue adequately. Adherence to tradition is of course fundamental to the Catholic faith, but development has always been part of tradition itself, so that in principle liturgists are justified in urging certain changes.

However, perhaps the single greatest liturgical error following the Council was to emphasize discontinuity, to speak continually of the "new" liturgy, and the consequent failure to make people understand how it was continuous with the old, a failure that is largely responsible for the movement that calls itself Traditionalism and that at its extremes has gone into schism.[25]

Liturgical change after the Council was originally justified as a return to the oldest liturgical forms, a program of "re-form" in which the ultimate criterion was the practice of the apostles. But innovators almost immediately found this to be inadequate and turned instead to contemporary culture as their primary inspiration. (This ambiguity remains. Catholics who express dissatisfaction with the reformed liturgy may be told either that the Church has returned to its ancient roots or that it has adapted itself to modern needs.)

Ritual embodies the entire history of a people and does so in such a way that their history remains alive, no matter how dimly they may understand it. In the words of Mary Douglas:

> We arise from the purging of old rituals simpler and poorer, as was intended, ritually beggared, but with other losses…Only a narrow range of historical experience is recognized as antecedent to the present state. Along with celebrating the Last Supper or the simplicity of fishermen-apostles, there is a squeamishness about ancestors…the anti-ritualists have rejected the list of saints and popes and tried to start again without the load of history.

The destruction of ritual "deprives men of the ability to articulate the depth of past time."[26] Pope Benedict has noted that, by appealing exclusively to the "early church" for justification, liturgists negated centuries of organic development and rendered those centuries irrelevant to the present.[27]

For some Catholics, the past of the Church has thus come to be a mere burden, even something shameful, and the seemingly irrational reactions of some people against anything traditional in liturgy—the compulsion to destroy old churches, for example—is an expression of that sense. Such things as Latin prayers, Gregorian chant, baroque polyphony, and gothic architecture arouse unease and even antagonism among some people, precisely because they speak of things that are mysterious, transcendent, and divine, demanding awe and reverence.

Authentic ritual has something about it that even appears archaic, which is not the equivalent of dead,[28] because such ritual is the experience of sacred time, of timelessness inside time.[29] While experimental liturgies purport to express human creativity—control over the world—in reality they reflect man's unfree place in that world because, in freeing themselves from the burdens of the past, modern men simply deliver themselves to the tyranny of history, often acting as though they have no right no live other than in accordance with the spirit of the times. Among other things, ritual embodies the deepest sense of order—the order of the cosmos itself—and when the rituals are in disarray the universe is experienced as disordered and man as trapped by the vagaries of chance and history.

The severing of continuity with tradition, whether deliberate or inadvertent, has had the result of throwing self-consciously modern Catholics entirely back on their own spiritual resources, which is a terrible kind of spiritual impoverishment. There is a direct link here to the heresy of Modernism, so named by St. Pius X because it is the only heresy in the history of the Church to impose a temporal obligation. All previous heresies laid claims to eternal truth; only Modernism demanded submission to the spirit of the age.

The experience of chaos is close to the heart of modernity, and the governing spirit of the broad cultural movement called Modernism can be defined as precisely the necessity of doubting even the possibility of ultimate transcendence, which makes the very idea of "modern" worship problematical. Many highly praised modern church buildings, for example, strike people as cold and empty. However impressive as architecture, they seem to speak not of God but almost of God's absence, of man as disoriented and embarked on some vague quest for "meaning." History shows that some ages are more creative than others, and it is inherently improbable that a self-consciously secular, in many ways even irreverent, culture like that of the present can create new religious forms of lasting value. Thus, until new forms of authentic liturgy reveal themselves, Catholics will of necessity look to the past, albeit not in that spirit of "restoration" or "retro" that substitutes for authentic tradition in our culture.

This rejection of the "burden" of the past not only leaves the individual imprisoned in the present, it also drastically truncates the worshipping community itself. No longer is the Mass celebrated in the presence of all the angels, as part of the Communion of Saints; it now becomes merely the activity of a particular group of people gathered in a particular time and place.

Not irrelevantly, there appears to be a steep decline in the practice of praying for the dead, due to a greatly diminished sense that living and dead are bound together in an eternal community. Ironically, the insistence that funeral liturgies be joyful celebrations of resurrection occurred at the moment when many people were losing their belief in personal resurrection, so that in practice Catholic funeral liturgies are now often mere celebrations of the life of the deceased, essentially secular memorial services inserted within the framework of a religious ritual.

Because the past is experienced as dead, the structure of the Church is of necessity also experienced as oppressive, so that "meaningful" religion necessarily involves the progressive rejection of doctrines and practices considered to be impositions on the self.

In times of radical change, ritual and symbol become sources of discord rather than of unity.[30] Instead of serving as an expression of a community's life, a ritual that is overly "relevant" can instead function as a further source of division.[31] After the Council both old things like Latin, Gregorian chant, and novenas, and newer things like banners and guitars, became bones of often rancorous contention.

Amidst the post-conciliar changes few mantras were intoned with as much reverence as "community," the achievement of which was said to be the chief purpose of change and the absence of which one of the chief failures of the pre-conciliar Church. But a living tradition is a vital part of every authentic community, so that the abandonment of so much tradition undermined the very goal that reformers ostensibly sought to achieve. The more the ideal of community was extolled, the more elusive it remained, to the point where for some people the local parish itself could no longer function as a community and they gathered for worship only with people of like mind, their refusal to participate in the ordinary rituals of the Church, their desire to find specialized celebrations (in either "liberal" or "conservative" versions), becoming a continuing symbol of the fragmentation of community.

Strong ritual, whose validity is implicitly accepted by everyone, is found in strong communities with a clear sense of their own boundaries—of how they differ from other groups—so that the weakening of community and the weakening of ritual symbiotically reinforce one another.[32] As traditionally understood by Catholics, community was not primarily a human entity, but was participation in the Communion of Saints, and the loss of that belief means that the inadequacies of particular communities cannot be transcended. As worshippers are urged to turn primarily towards one another, all divisions are magnified, to the point where only homogeneous communities are possible.

Once again a promise of freedom has led merely to a different kind of bondage, as the worshipper finds himself constrained not by the prescribed liturgy of the universal Church but by the arbitrary demands of a particular diocese or parish. Thus in the diocese of Orange [CA], parishioners in one parish have been told by their pastor that they commit a mortal sin by kneeling during the time of communion, a pronouncement supported by official diocesan spokesmen.[33]

The celebrant of the Mass is now often called the "presider," in order to minimize his hierarchical role and the idea that he represents Christ in some special way. But ironically, this has led to a new and exaggerated clericalism. In the traditional liturgy, the identity of the celebrant was largely irrelevant. But, as Max Weber pointed out, in times of confusion and destruction, authority shifts to the personality of the "charismatic leader," who appears to understand the movement of history and offers the guidance that established structures no longer provide.[34] As many commentators have noted, a possibly unintended affect of the celebrant's facing the people at Mass is to emphasize his personality and his "style" of celebration.

Interestingly, one of the first people to question the wisdom of this practice was the determinedly avant-garde communications theorist Marshall McLuhan, who warned that:

> A continuous confrontation of the audience by the celebrant
> reduces the occasion to a merely humanistic one..."Putting on"
> only the congregation as his corporate mark of dignity deprives
> the celebrant of any compelling power or charisma.[35]

Josef Jungmann, the magisterial historian of the liturgy, pointed out that it would be appropriate for the celebrant to face the people if the Mass were purely an act of instruction or celebration but not if it were "an immolation and homage to God,"[36] and the obscuring of the Mass as sacrifice has been perhaps the chief doctrinal danger posed by liturgical change. Pope Benedict himself has pointed out both the historical and theological fallacies of the *"versus populum"* position.[37]

Of all the deformations imposed in the Council's name, the most fundamental was the attempt to transform the essentially "vertical" act of worship—practically everything in the text of the Mass is directed to God, very little to one's neighbor—into a ritual of community fellowship, a prime example of Mary Douglas's "subverted symbol."

The ultimate root of liturgical disorder is a kind of popular, only half-understood version of the modern age's besetting heresy—Pelagianism—a denial of human sinfulness, as in the recent defiant assertion that worshippers at Mass should proclaim: "Jesus, I *am* worthy to receive you, help me to be more like you"! Then there is the equally defiant claim that official liturgy merely aims to "control" people.[38] While theological arguments can be made for standing during the most sacred parts of the Mass, many people now consider it actually demeaning to kneel in the presence of God.

Pelagianism expresses itself not only in such obvious ways but in a desire to make liturgy entirely a human creation, an emanation from the self, yet another manifestation of the individual's "creativity."

Thus the "style" of liturgy must now be elaborately and contrivedly casual, interlaced with attempts at humor, and with exchanges between celebrant and congregation replacing the homily, everything coordinated to effect an informal atmosphere in which people do not experience awe at being in the presence of the Almighty, and, above all, do they in no way feel themselves to be under judgment. For many people the greeting of peace, while a merely optional part of the liturgy, is nonetheless the high point of the celebration.[39] The ideal modern liturgy is celebrated in a secular space chosen merely for its convenience, with little that is distinctively religious—metal folding chairs, few if any sacred symbols, a minimum of priestly vestments, music scarcely distinguishable from what is heard on television, eucharistic vessels brought from the kitchen.

The endless debate over liturgical music is thus not merely about taste or quality. Quite early, advocates of the new music explicitly acknowledged that they intended to bring about an entirely new understanding of the nature of worship itself.[40] Although liturgists extol the necessity of "modern" music, in fact they ignore virtually the entire modernist movement in classical music—the pious Russian Orthodox Igor Stravinsky, for example—because such music is in many ways strange and demanding and does not provide the sense of cozy familiarity that comes from "folk music."

Overall, worship in the vernacular has been a benefit to the Church. But, along with a sense of sacred time, space, and gesture, a sense of sacred language has been one of the casualties of liturgical change. As the current debate over translations shows, liturgists for the most part ignore the fact that formal worship, in perhaps all the great religions of the world, has always been carried out in a sacred language, a language not necessarily incomprehensible to the worshippers but more formal and more archaic than their everyday idioms.

The poverty of post-conciliar liturgical language is not the result of mere insensitivity; it was designed to make the liturgical experience as mundane as possible. Even a general secretary of the ICEL at one time acknowledged that the translations were "feeble and hackneyed versions of the more powerful originals."[41]

In the end, eager participants in self-consciously "modern" liturgies want to hear only echoes of themselves, confirming Emile

Durkheim's claim that religion is finally the community objectifying and worshipping itself.[42]

The studied casualness of so much contemporary liturgy is itself an expression of fragmentation, because rituals of "solemn grandeur" must be performed in order to command the adherence of the entire community,[43] whereas casualness expresses the prevailing *Zeitgeist* and severely weakens the binding power that the ritual ought to have. If the prescribed liturgy of the Church is scrupulously observed in even the smallest communities, the worshippers are thereby united to the entire Communion of Saints.

The ultimate logical goal, towards which liturgical change has been moving with fits and starts for over forty years, is the suppression of ritual entirely, in the sense of structured symbolism, and its replacement by home-made, semi-spontaneous celebrations in which each community chooses the readings it finds most relevant to its needs and composes its own, possibly extemporaneous, prayers. Anything short of this cannot help but seem compromising to those who have interiorized the governing spirit of modern liturgy.

Along with this is a syncretism in which elements from a variety of traditions are cobbled together with little regard for their inherent significance, primarily in order to provide yet another "meaningful experience" for those who are alienated from their own traditions and for whom subjective experience alone retains the power to move. As Cardinal Francis Arinze has pointed out, in Africa ceremonial dance is not an expression of subjective "creativity," as it is likely to be in the West, but a formal and solemn ritual.[44]

The Liturgical Movement insisted that liturgy had to be relevant to life and hoped that liturgical reforms would undermine social evils, although the connection was seldom adequately explained. Liturgical renewal would prove itself in part by transforming Catholics into agents of social change.[45]

Immediately after the Council, in the fevered environment of "The Sixties," attempts were made to bring this about in direct ways that in effect denied the transcendent meaning of worship altogether, through homilies, unauthorized readings, and symbols directly related to social issues—efforts that fragmented the Liturgical Movement and persuaded some Catholics that worship itself was an irrelevant idea that distracted from social action. As Mary Douglas pointed out, once ritual has been declared meaningless and replaced by subjective experience, a move towards mere humanist philanthropy is inevitable, which means that "the symbolic life of the spirit is finished."[46]

But there is an even more fundamental question—why, within the context of certain influential schools of modern theology, should people feel bound to worship at all, in anything like the traditional sense, when such things as social action, the enjoyment of nature, or community celebrations might be more "meaningful" ways to God, however "God" is understood?

However, if human beings have an obligation to worship their creator, it follows that such worship is not ultimately validated by the worshippers themselves but must be a divine action they enter into, which in turn means that contemporary ideas of "meaningful" liturgy are in fact obstacles to authentic worship.

The time now seems ripe for the "reform of the reform," as Pope Benedict has called it, a process that looks hopeful, both because the Holy Father seems prepared to place the authority of his office behind it, and because at long last a majority of the American bishops not only seem to recognize the seriousness of the problems, but seem no longer willing to rely on the "experts" who caused most of those problems and tenaciously cling to the same mistaken ideas. Liturgy is the chief and most direct responsibility of the bishop—the principal manifestation of his office—and it is highly inappropriate that it should be delegated to bureaucrats. However, the liturgical bureaucracy is well-entrenched and has some episcopal support, as shown by the public resistance to the new liturgical translations.

As the Holy Father has also noted, a sweeping kind of reform, even if it moved in a good direction, would itself have a deeply upsetting affect on the community of the Church, comparable to that which followed the Council.[47] In the practical order it appears that the Church at this point has no alternative except to tolerate a kind of liturgical pluralism—continuing to insist on the obligation to observe the official rituals but within those limits allowing a variety of "styles," from the Tridentine Mass to the "guitar Mass." But although such a solution may be necessary, in this as in other areas, the Catholic Church now seems driven to adopt what is really the Anglican solution of attempting to minimize profound differences. For centuries the Church has encompassed a variety of rites, but the non-Roman rites were carefully circumscribed within particular communities with long traditions behind them, and Catholics were never permitted to join a particular rite merely on the basis of personal preference.

However, indirect the process of renewal may turn out to be, our goals must remain clear, so that over what will probably be a period of decades rather than of years the movement of authentic reform may succeed. There is at present no grounds for exuberance, but perhaps only for the dry comfort that Winston Churchill offered the British people in 1942: "This not the end. It is not even the beginning of the end. But perhaps it is the end of the beginning."

James Hitchcock is a professor of history at St. Louis University, where he has taught since 1966. A native St. Louisan, he received a PhD in history from Princeton University, and before returning to St. Louis taught at St. John's University in New York. A founding member and past president of the Fellowship of Catholic Scholars, he received the organization's Cardinal Wright Award in 1981. He was the first editor of the American edition of *Communio: International Catholic Review* (1974-1982) and was also chairman of its editorial board (1982-1984).

Dr. Hitchcock is the author of many books, including *Catholicism and Modernity* (1979) and *Recovery of the Sacred* (1974), and, most recently, a two-volume work, *The Supreme Court and Religion in American Life* (2004). He also recently completed an intellectual biography of Christopher Dawson. His many articles and essays have appeared in numerous Catholic and secular publications; he writes a regular column for the Catholic press; and he serves on the editorial boards of both *Touchstone* magazine and the *Human Life Review*. He is married to Helen Hull Hitchcock and is the father of four daughters (and is now a grandfather of four). With his wife, he served as program co-chairman for this 29th annual FCS convention as well as keynote speaker.

Endnotes

[1] How the goals of the classical Liturgical Movement in effect became reversed— whether liturgists were already planning a revolution before the Council, or whether their agenda was transformed in the frenzied atmosphere that immediately followed— is unclear. For clues see Kathleen Hughes, *The Monk's Tale* (Collegeville, Mn., 1991), a biography of the strategically situated Benedictine liturgist Godfrey Diekmann.

[2] *The Revival of Liturgy* (New York, 1963), 208, 211-2, 218.

[3] Gerard Sloyan, *Worship in a New Key* (New York, 1965), 16-7, 22-5,68-9, 71, 139, 172-8.

[4] Landon G. Dowdey, in *Worship in the City of Man,* ed. Daniel O'Hanlon, S.J. (The Liturgical Conference, 1966), 163, 167.

[5] Victor Turner, "Passages, Margins, and Poverty," *Worship,* XLVI, 7 (September, 1972), 398.

[6] Francis W. Mahoney, M.M., "The Aymara Indians: Model for Ritual Adaptation," *Worship, XLV,* 67 (Aug.-Sept., 1971), 407.

[7] In particular, see the "spirituality" of the former Dominican Matthew Fox: *On Becoming a Musical, Mystical Bear* (New York, 1972) and Creation Spirituality (San Francisco, 1991).

[8] A.R. Radcliffe-Brown, *Structure and Function in Primitive Society* (Glencoe, Ill, 1952), 157. While there are immense differences between pagan and Christian ritual and between "primitive" and sophisticated cultures, ritual, like art, music, and other things incorporated into worship, retains certain common characteristics across those boundaries. While the Catholic liturgy obviously transcends all other rituals, it is assumed here that on one level it can be understood as an example of such ritual and that many of the most serious errors of liturgical reform stemmed from a failure to understand the nature of ritual, even on the purely human level.

[9] Mary Douglas, *Natural Symbols* (New York, 1970), 1-2, 8, 11, 47.

[10] Concerning the clerical mind on these matters, see Ibid., 50.

[11] *Ibid.,* 9, 38.

[12] *The Folk Culture of Yucatan* (Chicago, 1955), 363.

[13] See, for example, the numerous examples in James Hitchcock, *The Recovery of the Sacred* (New York, 1979).

[14] For a description of how the effort to "purify" religion can lead to its weakening, see William A. Christian, *Person and God in a Spanish Valley* (New York, 1972), 161, 178, 184-7.

[15] Clifford Geertz, "Religion as a Cultural System," *The Religious Situation:* 1968, ed. Donald R. Cutler (Boston, 1968), 642.

[16]On this point see Douglas, *Natural Symbols,* 147.

[17]*The Spirit of the Liturgy,* tr. John Saward (San Francisco, 2000), 168. See also Cardinal Francis Arinze, "Liturgical Norms and Liturgical Piety," *Adoremus Bulletin,* XI, 3 (May, 2005).

[18]Gerald Sigler, quoted by William McKaye, in *The Washington Post,* Nov. 16, 1973, D18. Sigler later left the priesthood.

[19]Louis Bouyer, *Liturgical Piety* (Notre Dame, Ind., 1954), 8; Turner, "Passages, Margins, and Poverty," 400.

[20]Emile Durkheim, *The Elementary Forms of Religious Life,* tr. Joseph Ward Swayne (New York, 1961), 41; Redfield, Folk Culture, 311. See also Arinze, "Liturgical Norms."

[21]"Liturgy and Spiritual Personalism," *Worship,* XXXIV, 9 (October, 1960), 503-5

[22]Turner, "Subjectivity and Objectivity in Theology and Worship," *Worship,* XLI, 3 (March, 1967), 160. Although *Worship* published several of Turner's critiques of liturgical change, there is no evidence that his ideas were ever heeded.

[23]Geertz, "Religion as Cultural System," 643, 649-50.

[24]For a remarkably candid acknowledgement of this, see Ralph Keifer, "Ritual Makers and Poverty of Proclamation," *Worship,* XLVI, 2 (January, 1972), 69-75. Keifer was general secretary of ICEL. One of the minor mysteries of the post-conciliar period is the fact that, although from time to time *Worship* itself published perceptive analyses of liturgical fallacies, none of these seem ever to have made the slightest impression on the architects of change.

[25]The movement can be followed in the pages of the newspaper *The Remnant.*

[26]*Natural Symbols,* 19-20

[27]*Spirit of Liturgy,* 82-4.

[28]Turner, "Passages, Margins, and Poverty," 391-2.

[29]Mircea Eliade, *The Sacred and the Profane,* tr. Willard R. Trask (New York, 1961), 68, 85, 89; Turner, "Passages, Margins, and Poverty," 399.

[30]Geertz, "Ritual and Social Change," *American Anthropologist,* XLIX, 1 (February, 1957), 32-54.

[31]Turner, "Passages, Margins, and Poverty," 398. In the Orange controversy (see note 33), Bishop Todd Brown pointed out that, while some parishioners protested the liturgical rules decreed by their new pastor, others welcomed them as overdue.

[32]Douglas, *Natural Symbols,* 13-4, 19, 30, 33, 35, 139, 141.

[33]The pastor subsequently amended his pronouncement from "mortal sin" to "an objectively serious matter." While acknowledging that it was improper to characterize kneeling as a mortal sin, Bishop Todd Brown scolded parishioners for their liturgical intransigence and regretted that the diocese had erred in the past by treating them overly indulgently. (See the *Los Angeles Lay Catholic Mission,* Sept.-Oct., 2006, for a detailed account of the controversy. Bishop Brown's letter to the parish appears on www.renewAmeica.us/columns/abbott for September 14, 2006.) For Pope Benedict's justification for kneeling at Mass, see Spirit of Liturgy, 184-5.

34The *Theory of Economic and Social Organization,* ed. Talcott Parsons (Glencoe, Ill, 1947), 361

[35]"Liturgy and Media," *The Critic,* XXXI, 4 (Mar.-Apr., 1973), 70.

[36]*The Mass of the Roman Rite,* tr. Francis A. Brunner, C.Ss.R. (New York, 1959), 181-2

[37]*Spirit of Liturgy,* 63-7.

[38]Joe Droste (letter), *National Catholic Reporter,* July 28, 2006, 20.

[39]For examples of extreme attempts at "creative" liturgies, see Hitchcock, *Recovery of the Sacred,* especially 48-9, 61-2.

[40]For example, Robert W. Hovda and Gabe Huck, "Music: We Must Learn to Celebrate," *Liturgical Arts,* XXXVIII, 2 (February, 1970), 4.

[41]Keifer, "Squalor on Sunday," *Worship,* XLIV, 5 (May, 1970), 293.

[42]*Elementary Forms,* 474-9.

[43]Bronlislaw Malinowski, *Magic, Science, and Religion* (Garden City, N.Y., 1955), 67.

[44]"On 'Liturgical Dance,'" *Adoremus Bulletin,* XI, 3 (May, 2005).

[45]This was, for example, the strongly held position of Dom Virgil Michel, O.S.B., the founder of *Orate Fratres* (later *Worship*) magazine. See Paul Marx, O.S.B., *Virgil Michel and the Liturgical Movement* (Collegeville, Mn., 1957)

[46]*Natural Symbols,* 7, 31, 42.

[47]*Spirit of Liturgy,* 83.

II.

ADDRESS TO THE FELLOWSHIP

To The Heart
of the Mystery

Archbishop Malcolm Ranjith

It is my great pleasure to send greetings to all who are taking part in the 29th Annual Convention of the Fellowship of Catholic Scholars, and especially so since you have chosen on this occasion for your theme "*Sacrosanctum Concilium* and the Reform of the Liturgy".

The very mention of the Liturgy takes us to the heart of the sacred mystery, which in the first place is not a goal that the men and women of our fevered and pragmatic age set themselves to reach, but the pure and unimaginable gift of God, bestowed upon us along the inscrutable highways and by-ways of our personal histories.

Already the very fact of our existence in this wonderful world prompts us to direct our gaze to the heavens and to utter our hymn of praise. But the supreme motive of our thanksgiving is the relentless action of God's grace, the course as it were of Francis Thompson's "hound of heaven," pursuing us along the inscrutable highways and by-ways of our personal histories and pointing us, nuzzling us, sometimes almost frightening us in the direction of a mountain that all must climb, Mount Calvary where Christ Jesus our Lord has been raised up between heaven and earth, drawing all the sons and daughters of God's adoption to himself.

It is to this pinnacle of Calvary that the conciliar Constitution on the Sacred Liturgy, *Sacrosanctum Concilium*, takes us. And that is true in various senses.

Firstly, of course, we recall that pithily expressed intuition that the sacred Liturgy is the fountainhead and culmination (*fons et culmen)* of the whole of the Church's activity, an intuition that was then applied in other documents of the Council and the popes in a special way to the celebration of Holy Mass,

Then, the Constitution *Sacrosanctum Concilium* proved to be itself, providentially, in some sense a fountainhead and culmination, or at least a starting point and point of conclusion. For the work on the Constitution on the Sacred Liturgy served to lead the Fathers into the work of the Council and to orientate them by means of a debate and study that, while concentrating on the specific question of the Liturgy, also opened up a pastoral vista of the interplay between the eternal truths of faith, our understanding of them at the successive moments of God's grace, and the challenges we face in an ever-changing age to further the sanctification of the world. In that sense, the Constitution *Sacrosanctum Concilium*, like the Liturgy it treats, is certainly a fruitful point of departure for a constantly renewed attempt to understand the theology of the Church, its mission and pastoral action.

I may permit myself here to note in an aside the great importance I see in another affirmation of *Sacrosanctum Concilium*, namely, that the celebration of the Liturgy does not exhaust the activity of the Church. Doubtless the Council Fathers intended to recall those wonderful words of Saint Paul to the Romans, that in order for the world to have faith, and—we might add—for that faith to be celebrated in the Eucharist, the faith has to be preached to them, through all the channels of human communication. With hindsight we can link this affirmation to the damage done by the uncomprehending in some places in their attempts to lever into the Liturgy everything from talent contests to political debate, thus almost squeezing out the essential, the mystery of God.

It was perhaps an easy temptation to seize upon the Liturgy Constitution as a rough-and-ready manual, a sort of loose-leaf binder of instructions of the kind that used to accompany children's toy construction sets. My own view is that far from being the triumph of pragmatism, the Liturgy Constitution reveals more of its true self if it is read as a "mystical" document, one that opens the eyes of faith, the eyes of the Church, to an enrapturing vision of what the Liturgy naturally is. It seems to me that *Sacrosanctum Concilium* most importantly plays the chords of a marvelous sacred symphony of the truth as expressed in the different books of the divine Scriptures, from the evangelistic longings of Isaiah, to the cosmic ecclesiology of the Letters to the Colossians and the Ephesians, to the irruption of God's light and love in the Johannine writings, to the sacrificial theology of Christ the Eternal High Priest in the Letter to the Hebrews, all as it were caught up into the great panorama of the Book of the Apocalypse, linking as it does the definitive victory of the Son of God over all evil with the outplaying of the drama of the heavenly Liturgy.

The action of the Holy See, likewise, important as it is, cannot exhaust the activity of the Church. It is all the more urgent that gatherings such as yours assist by their labors and prayers the pastors and the bishops to glimpse the heart of the mystery, so that throughout the Church we can all be open in every age to its self-revelation.

The Holy See has been engaged with the bishops in drawing attention to the singular importance of the Sacrament of Sacraments, the wondrous Sacrament of the Most Blessed Eucharist, in unfolding an understanding of its treasures and in safeguarding them from the abusive inroads of superficiality and arbitrariness, oftentimes a result of yielding to the temptation for "quick results." It is singular how in the encyclical *Ecclesia de Eucharistia* the late Pope John Paul II stresses so delicately and yet so powerfully the dimension of "awe" or "astonishment" that the Eucharist should inspire in the Church as a whole and in the individual believer. This deep sense of "awe" does help us to achieve an attitude of silence and listening and engaging in a "conversational attitude" before the Lord.This is to be always cultivated.

Besides, the Holy See has also launched a wide campaign to ensure that the liturgical life of the Church be given more importance and that everything be carried on with an even greater sense of seriousness. It is good to see that with the assistance of the world's bishops, this campaign is gradually bearing fruit. The Holy See is also engaged with the struggle to ensure that the translations of the Liturgy in the various authorized languages convey faithfully that astonishing web of words of wisdom that the Fathers of the Church by their contemplation and pastoral experience drew from the Sacred Scriptures and fashioned to be the Church's expression of faith in the course of liturgical celebration. This was the Council's intention, and now, correcting our sights through experience, I believe we are making progress towards improvement in this area too.

In two other areas to which your gathering intends to dedicate attention, that of sacred art and architecture, and that of sacred music, the interventions of the Holy See have, shall we say, been less programmatic, even if the basic principles have been steadily and repeatedly invoked. Since in both these sectors the true path has not rarely in practice been lost from view, there is wide scope for the investment of further energy in a way that starts with deepened reflection on the realities of the faith and on the effective needs of liturgical celebration.

I should like to draw a certain connection between the promotion of authentic sacred art and sacred music on the one hand, and what has happened, on the other, in the matter of Eucharisitic adoration, where we have seen in recent years a groundswell of spontaneous commitment on the part of so many Catholic families and individual laypeople in so many regions of the world. These families did not wait for the Holy See to issue new documents, but rather pressed their priests to provide for their needs according to the existing provisions. They have organized groups, they have published and disseminated hymnals and prayer books. I know that many of you who take part in this gathering have given your energies to this holy enterprise, and have been richly rewarded.

It seems to me, on the one hand, that the time is right for those who have even modest natural talent in the fields of sacred art and sacred music to engage under the action of God's grace in promoting a renewal in the parishes. The products taken up, packaged, and commercialized in these years have not always been happily devised, either in visual art, in the form and adornment of our churches, or in the kind of music introduced into the Liturgy. On the other hand, when true art has emerged, visual or musical, it has often too easily been shunted off into what is in effect the world of the art exhibition or the concert, a product to provoke our applause of the artist rather than thanksgiving to Almighty God.

Prompted by that notion of "noble simplicity" that the Council Fathers made their own in *Sacrosanctum Concilium* (34), it is time for us to take stock of our patrimony, but also to make a gift to God of the talents and the cultural currents of our time among all the different peoples in whom the Gospel has taken root. Incidentally, we can begin to draw encouragement from the freshness and spontaneity of the short occasional messages and addresses which our Holy Father Pope Benedict has addressed to choirs and musical gatherings since his election.

My recent appointment by the Holy Father as Secretary of the Congregation for Divine Worship and the Discipline of the Sacraments assigns me an institutional role in these questions within the activity of the Holy See, but perhaps you see between the lines of my message that my interest in the Liturgy is far from a merely formal one. Having been privileged to serve as diocesan bishop and to serve in areas of the world where Catholic life is not always easy, I have seen at first hand how the Church's stress on the crucial importance of the Liturgy rings true.

The fact of your faithfully organizing a meeting on these matters, as in the past you have done on other realities of Catholic life, does you all great credit and is a clear sign of hope. It augurs well for the Church. I send you my warmest personal wishes for a successful convention, accompanied by the sincere assurance of my prayers.

May God bless you all!

Archbishop Malcolm Ranjith Patabendige Don is currently the secretary of the Congregation for Divine Worship and the Discipline of the Sacraments in Rome. He is a native of Sri Lanka, born there on November 15, 1947. He studied philosophy at the National Major Seminary in Kandy beginning in 1966, and then, in 1971, he entered the Urban College in Rome where he completed his theological studies. He was ordained a priest of the archdiocese of Colombo in June, 1975, by Pope Paul VI. He filled several pastoral assignments in Sri Lanka, and, in 1982, he was additionally named to be the director of the diocesan Caritas organization. Between 1983 and 1993 he was national director of the Pontifical Mission Works in Sri Lanka.

He was appointed to be an auxiliary bishop of Colombo in 1991. In 1995, a new diocese of Ratnapura was formed and he was appointed to be its first bishop. Around the same time, he became secretary general of the Sri Lanka bishops' conference and chairman of its Justice and Peace Commission. In 2001 he was appointed to be the adjunct secretary of the Congregation for the Evangelization of Peoples in Rome. Subsequently, he served as apostolic nuncio to Indonesia and East Timor. Finally, on December 10, 2005, Pope Benedict XVI appointed him to be the secretary of the Congregation for Divine Worship and the Discipline of the Sacraments, where he took up his duties in February, 2006. Archbishop Ranjith's address reprinted here was read *in absentia.*

III.

In Pursuit of an *Ars Celebrandi*: Presuppostions And Possibilities

Rev. Msgr. James P. Moroney

In the spring of 2001, the Congregation for Divine Worship and the Discipline of the Sacraments met in plenary session to consider the major questions before the church in this period of the post-conciliar liturgical renewal. It is significant that among the major issues up for discussion by the bishop members was the idea of *ars celebrandi*, a subject addressed at some length by Cardinal George Pell. His Eminence stressed that for the priest in particular, *ars celebrandi* is not only a matter of preparation of mind, body, and heart, but also an appreciation of the gestures, the attitude of the body, and the dignity of a humble leadership that is evident to the people in a man who is loving and able to pray the liturgy, able not only to cover himself in sacred vestments, but above all, to be clothed with the Lord Jesus Christ.

His Eminence's emphasis on the *ars celebrandi* is an echo of an entirely new paragraph in the *General Instruction* of the third edition of the *Missale Romanum*, published the year before the *plenarium*. Paragraph 93 presents a job description of the priest at Mass, who because he "possesses within the Church the power of Holy Orders to offer sacrifice in the person of Christ, stands...at the head of the faithful people gathered together here and now, presides over their prayer, proclaims the message of salvation to them, associates the people with himself in the offering of sacrifice through Christ in the Holy Spirit to God the Father, gives his brothers and sisters the Bread of eternal life, and partakes of it with them." What is particularly interesting, however, is that this job description is followed by a performance review, perhaps one of the most succinct and challenging statements ever written of who the priest is supposed to be at Mass: "When he celebrates the Eucharist, therefore, he must serve God and the people with dignity and humility, and by his bearing and by the way he says the divine words he must convey to the faithful the living presence of Christ" (*General Instruction of the Roman Missal*, 93).

Is there any more important agenda in the renewal of the liturgical reform of the Second Vatican Council than fostering from the inside out a true appreciation of this *ars celebrandi* in the heart of every priest? I mean an *ars celebrandi* which is not so much a matter of mastering skills, as conforming my heart to the Lord into whose Priesthood I have been ordained, and with whom I seek to join his holy people?

The Council Fathers first articulated this truth in the oft-quoted fourteenth paragraph of the conciliar Constitution *Sacrosanctum Concilium.* Have you ever listened to a talk on the sacred Liturgy which has not recalled that the "full and active participation by all the people is the aim to be considered before all else..."? However, seldom is the paragraph quoted in context. For this seminal challenge is immediately followed by the strikingly blunt assertion that it "would be futile to entertain any hopes of realizing this unless the pastors themselves, in the first place, become thoroughly imbued with the spirit and power of the liturgy" (SC 14)

Over the past several years I have spoken to almost 20,000 priests and deacons in eighty-six dioceses about conforming their hearts to Christ and engaging in a renewal of the sacred Liturgy from the inside out. Seldom, however, are they reminded that they, as pastors of souls, are the agents whom the Fathers of the Second Vatican Council envisioned as the primary agents of the liturgical reform. The success or failure of the conciliar vision is largely in their hands. And success must always begin with a renewal of their priestly hearts.

Our Holy Father, Pope Benedict XVI, his frequently returned to this theme, as he did in a recent conversation with Italian diocesan priests. The *ars celebrandi*, he insisted, first demands that "the priest enter truly into [the dialogue between God and man, which is at the heart of the sacred Liturgy]. Announcing the Word, he must feel himself in colloquy with God."

Of course, we might be tempted to reply. Every priest knows that when he stands at the altar he is in dialogue with God. But does he? Is the focus of the average American priest at mass more on Christ or on the performative and relational dimensions of the ritual he has been taught to enact? Are the individual relational aspects of his art sometimes prior to and obstructive of the divine dialogue into which he is called to lead us?

"He is in a dialogue with God," the Holy Father reminds us, precisely "because the texts of the Holy Mass are not theatrical lines or some such—they are prayers, thanks to which, together with the congregation, I as priest talk to God."

Pope Benedict XVI then introduces us to the mystagogical dimension of the *ars celebrandi*, recalling how the Rule of Saint Benedict describes the monk's praying of the Psalms as "*Mens concordet voci*." So too with all the words and rites of the sacred Liturgy, they begin with an enacted or spoken prayer, and only then invite us to enter into their meaning, to join the dialogue with God.

Such a mystagogical approach to the Liturgy, the Holy Father suggests, demands that we approach the Sacred Mysteries as "a continuation of a permanent growth in adoration and in announcing the Gospel...so that we might enter and join our minds and hearts to the voice of the Church."

Thus do we "transform our "I" into the "we' of the Church, enriching and amplifying this "I," praying with the Church, with the words of the Church, and being truly in colloquy with God."

Notice the Holy Father's constant insistence on internalization as the first prerequisite for an authentic priestly *ars celebrandi*. A few years ago, I was invited by the Cathedral Rectors' Association to address them on how to improve cathedral Liturgy. While they were probably expecting a dissertation on the fine points of the latest rubrical disputes, that's not what they got. For to make better priest celebrants, I suggested to them, you need to encourage priests to be holier: to seek after sanctity, to long for prayer, to rejoice in virtue, to be conformed more and more to Christ. That is the secret of the *ars celebrandi*: obedience, authentitcity, humility, and love for the sacred rites and texts are by-products of a life lived in close communion with Christ. It is the same secret known by Chaucer in the Parson's tale: "Christe's lore and his apostles twelve he taught...but first he followed it himself."

While the recently promulgated third edition of the Roman Missal speaks convincingly of the priest's responsibility to adapt the sacred Liturgy to the genius and culture of each individual gathered assembly, we perhaps sometimes forget that, in the words of Cardinal Francis Arinze, such exterior engagement is drawn from and is based upon a deep and interior relationship with Christ. "On the one hand, he cannot isolate himself from the presence of the people. On the other hand, he should not become a showman who projects himself." "The Liturgy," he stressed, "is not primarily what we make but what we receive in faith" (11th General Synod of Bishops, session eight).

Nor is this theme unique to the present pontificate. It was Pope John Paul II who encouraged priests never to forget the "intimate bond between the priest's spiritual life and the exercise of his ministry" (*Pastores Dabo Vobis*, 24). And the same pontiff who issued perhaps the most challenging words of the first forty years of the liturgical reform, when he reminded the bishops of the United States in the course of their *ad limina* visit that "prayer for the needs of the Church and the individual faithful is so important that serious thought should be given to reorganizing priestly and parish life to ensure that priests have time to devote to this essential task, individually and in common. Liturgical and personal prayer, not the tasks of management, must define the rhythms of a priest's life, even in the busiest of parishes" (May 21, 1998, Pope John Paul H to bishops from Michigan and Ohio during their *ad limina* visit to the Holy See).

Would that we would heed those prescient words! But why don't we? Is it because we share in an American obsession with doing over being, with relating over reflecting, with performance over substance, with pleasure over patience, with satisfaction over truth? Is it because we fear the silent, the reflective, the quiet presence of God in the heart of a listening child?

We live in a society which loves to "get things done." We are great "doers." Thus we are able to embrace with gusto the aspect of the liturgical reform which called us to "do more." But we're not so good at reflecting, at meditating on the mysteries we celebrate. Without such meditation, without a life of reflective prayer, we will never be able to celebrate the Mass fully, consciously, or actually.

Perhaps this is why we have experienced such resistance to quiet prayer before the Blessed Sacrament. The kind of quiet worship espoused by Pope Paul VI, when he wrote: "Dwelling with Christ our Lord, they enjoy his intimate friendship and pour out their hearts before him for themselves and their dear ones, and pray for the peace and salvation of the world. They offer their entire lives with Christ to the Father in the Holy Spirit, and receive in this wonderful exchange an increase of faith, hope and charity. Thus they nourish those right dispositions which enable them with all due devotion to celebrate the memorial of the Lord and receive frequently the bread given us by the Father."

I remember one of the first times this truth came home to me. It was one night after I had been in the parish for only a few months. Around 2 a.m. I got a sick-call from the daughter of a woman who was dying half way across town. I made my way to the house, as you have done so many times, blinking furiously to try to awaken my body. I anointed the woman, gave her viaticum, and prayed with the family for a short time, after which, by the grace of God, the woman died. As I drove back to the rectory I knew I would not be able to fall asleep again right away, so I went to the adoration chapel.

I entered and knelt down behind an old man who was praying from a tattered devotional. He got up and left and was replaced by a giant of a man. In early middle age, this man had the shoulders of a Green Bay Packer and enormous hands—rough and leathery and swollen from years of hard physical labor. In soiled work clothes he had obviously just come off second shift and was stopping by the chapel for his hour of prayer.

As he knelt there, he placed his head in those swollen hands and did not move for the next hour. All I could hear was a slight muttering of prayer, an echo of his intimate conversation with the God in whom he found his only rest.

How, then, can a priest approach the sacred mysteries, speak the sacred texts, or give his body, mind, and voice over to the immemorial rights unless he is willing to seek the secret of this mystery in the silent beauty of the God who whispers to his heart? If the priest is not passionately in love with Christ and the sacred rites which join us to his Sacred Heart, if he is unwilling or unable to empty his heart in the same way that Christ died for him on the cross, then how can he take up the cup of salvation and call upon the name of the Lord?

For the secret, you see, is in three little words spoken to the priest when the chalice filled with wine and that paten with bread are first placed into his hands: *agnosce, imitare, conforma*: know what you are doing, imitate what you touch, and conform your life to the cross. I suggest that these mandates describes a radically new and challenging way of relating to the Liturgy and plot a certain course for growing in the *ars celebrandi.*

Agnosce

Hear the Council Fathers on this: Pastors of souls must therefore realize that, when the liturgy is celebrated, something more is required than the mere observation of the laws governing valid and licit celebration; it is their duty also to ensure that the faithful take part fully aware of what they are doing, actively engaged in the rite, and enriched by its effects (SC 11).

Notice the phrase is "something more...than valid and licit celebration." The presumption here is that the Liturgy is celebrated in full accordance with the laws of the Roman rite. As one liturgist is wont to say, people have a right to the Roman Rite! It is a rite whose immemorial Liturgy is always far more appropriate than the private musings or personal adaptations made by a charismatically inspired individual, even if he is a priest. Or, as *Sacrosanctum Concilium* put it so well, "no other person, not even a priest, may add, remove, or change anything in the liturgy on his own authority" (SC 22.3).

The first requirement of the priest who seeks to conform himself to Christ in celebrating the sacred Liturgy is to faithfully, obediently, and authentically seek to sing God's praise in tune with the Church. This is the message of *Redemptionis Sacramentum,* of the extraordinary efforts of the bishops of this country to promote a faithful implementation of the *General Instruction of the Roman Missal* and the continuing efforts of the Bishops' Committee and the Liturgy in this regard.

Imitare

We are called to be transformed by the sacred mysteries we celebrate, to imitate the very mysteries we touch. Such change, however, can only be the result of a profound appreciation of the Scriptures, a typological mystagogy which enters deeply into the language and the life of the sacred Liturgy and its rites and texts.

When a priest picks up the chalice at Mass, how can this change him? If he sees this sacred vessel simply as a cup to be raised to prescribed heights and over which he must sing or say prescribed formulas, I suggest that not much will happen to him. However:

- If in the quiet of his room late at night he meditates on the cup of suffering which the Lord prayed would pass him by (Mt 26:39); or on the "cup of blessing," of which St. Paul writes;
- If each day, in the name of Jesus, he offers to those in need that "cup of cold water" of which our Savior spoke (Mk 9:4);
- If before the Blessed Sacrament he recalls the life-giving "cup of the new and everlasting covenant" (Lk 22:20);
- If when he looks upon Christ on the cross he see a chalice, emptied that we might be filled, "obedient unto death, death on a cross" (Phil 2:7-8);
- If the priest then comes to understand deeply the chalice that he holds in his hands—then he too will become a chalice: ready to be emptied, ready like Christ, to learn through obedience to the will of the Father. (Heb.5.8).

A true understanding of what it means to take that sacred chalice in my hands gives me the grace to accept the kind of suffering I would instinctively shun, even as Jesus did in the garden (Mk 14:36). For most assuredly, in our own Gethsemenes, we will find this same chalice offered to us over and over again, until we have drunk it fully and thereby been "conformed to the image" (Rom 8:29) of Christ. Each day, then, as we raise that chalice at Mass, we can make our own the words of Psalm 116, so appropriately incorporated into the offertory of the old Dominican rite: "What return shall I make to the Lord for all the good things he has done for me The cup of salvation I will take up, and I will call upon the name of the Lord."

By rite and by life, then, the priest is called to conform his life to him in whose image he acts ay Mass. The priest who seeks to conform himself to the paschal Christ must ever pray for the gifts of humility and obedience: Obedience to the prayer of the Church, obedience to the word of God which calls him to die to himself in the model of Christ, and obedience to the Sacred Euchology and Sacred rites he prays. Such an obedience makes of the priest presiding at the liturgy a humble servant.

He is not a host, like Oprah Winfrey: his success is not gauged by how entertained people feel. He is not a performer: his success is not gauged by how much he stirs human emotions. He is not a politician: his success is not gauged by how popular he is.

He is a servant-priest in the likeness of Christ Jesus, whose success is gauged by how transparently he shows forth Christ, how effectively he leads people to Christ, and how obediently he dies to himself so that it is no longer he who lives but Christ Jesus who lives in him—no longer he who is seen, but Christ Jesus who is alive and acting and present to his Church through him.

Such is the goal not only of a presbyteral *ars celebrandi*, but of the whole liturgical reform and of the whole Christian life. As we attempt to breathe new life into that reform, the indispensable imperative is to seek for holiness, to pray, to live virtuously, to readily forgive, and to always speak the truth. Saint Ignatius of Antioch knew this to be true to his very last breath, when he urged us to center on the essentials and not be distracted: he urged us to keep out eyes on the prize:

> At worship, you must be like the strings of a lyre, each in harmony with the bishops. Hence it is that in the harmony of your minds and hearts Jesus Christ is hymned. Make of yourselves a choir, so that with one voice and one mind, taking the key-note of God, you may sing in unison with one voice through Jesus Christ to the Father, and He may hear you and recognize you...as members of his Son.

Monsignor James P. Moroney, a priest of the Diocese of Worcester, Massachusetts, is Executive Director of the Secretariat for the Liturgy of the United States Conference of Catholic Bishops (USCCB). He has pursued theological studies at the Pontifical Gregorian University, the Pontifical Liturgy Institute at San Anselmo's in Rome and at the Catholic University of America.

Past Chairman of the Federation of Diocesan Liturgical Commissions, he came to the Bishops' Committee on the Liturgy in 1996, after having served for fifteen years as a parish priest and pastor. In 1999 and 2004, Pope John Paul II appointed him to five-year terms as a consultor to the Congregation for Divine Worship and the Discipline of the Sacraments. He is the fourth American liturgist to be appointed to this post since the Second Vatican Council. He also serves as a advisor to the *Vox Clara* Committee of that same Congregation. A popular lecturer on the subject of the liturgy, Monsignor Moroney has spoken to some 18,000 priests and deacons at the invitation of more than 80 diocesan bishops over the past few years.

IV.

Session I
Musicam Sacram

Sacred Music in a 12th-Century Monastery:
Any Lessons for Us Nowadays?

Rev. Chrysogonus Waddell, O. S. C. O.

At the very end of the 11th century a group of twenty-one monks and their father abbot set out from their flourishing monastery of Molesme, in the diocese of Langres, France. They were headed for a swampy bit of property called Cîteaux, not many miles distant from Dijon.The challenge they faced was a considerable one. There they hoped to found a monastery in which the Rule of St. Benedict could be observed in its integrity, without undue accretions or mitigations. But they were also much concerned for a return to the sources for every aspect of their life, and this touched largely on their liturgy and the music with which they celebrated the liturgy. We, too, in the aftermath of Vatican II, are also faced, liturgically, with enormous challenges. My own conviction is that we who are concerned for, and who love the liturgy and sacred music, have much that we could learn from those twelfth-century monks.

First of all, almost every literate individual in the twelfth century had at least a hazy general idea about the nature of music based on a few texts by the early (fifth to sixth century) Christian philosopher Boethius. For Boethius and the twelfth-century monk, there were *three* kinds of music. One of these was what Boethius called *musica humana*, "music of humans," and I wish to dwell on this kind of music for a moment or two. *Musica humana* meant that inner principle of harmony unifying body and soul with all one's interior faculties; and it was from this interior order based on truth and beauty that outward action was to proceed. There is a wonderful responsory from St. Bernard's Night Office, composed a bit before 1174, that illustrates this wonderfully well. The text is impossible to translate; but let me give you at least an approximate idea of what it says.

The responsory begins this way: "The first virtue of the holy man was the *habitus* of his body—and *habitus* means not just Bernard's posture, and not just how he used his body as an instrument of expression, but his body itself as an expression of the fullness of his interior life: body-language in the deepest meaning of the term. We next read that Bernard acted *composite*. *Composite* is a wonderful word. It comes from the verb *componere*, "to piece or fit together." In other words, St. Bernard "had it all together." Everything he did and said formed a harmonious, coherent, beautiful whole. So also he acted always *uno modo*, in a uniformly consistent manner, in which exterior expression was like music springing from an interior principle. Everything within him was *disciplinatum*, in perfect order, functioning at its optimum; everything about him was *insigne virtutis*, a sign, an expression of his inner strength and virtue and spiritual beauty; everything about him was *perfectionis forma*, a model of perfection, an example of what it means to be a fully, completely 'achieved' human being. This entire responsory, then, is about *musica humana*, that unifying principle which makes music of one's whole being. Does this have any relevance for us moderns, distracted and torn in umpteen different directions, as we tend to be?

As for Boethius' *musica intrumentalis*, that is, music produced by human instruments and voices, "instrumental music" was simply the material expression in sounding ratios and proportions of realities of a higher and deeper order. It is against this background that we have to understand the monk's passion for music theory and mathematics. The monk would have agreed with Edna Saint-Vincent Millay, who once wrote that "Euclid alone has looked on beauty bare." This conviction led St. Bernard and his colleagues to revise the entire traditional chant repertory on the basis of norms taken from the more prominent music theorists of the Middle Ages. We moderns may rightly regret this naïve confidence placed in music theorists, but the intention of these Cistercians was laudable in the extreme: they meant to restore the allegedly corrupt chants to their original, pristine nature in keeping with their own inner truth; for only thus could this music be authentic music, reflecting the order of the divinely created cosmos, and fostering the restoration of our native inward harmony thrown into disorder by the effects of sin. For the Cistercians, a badly constructed melody is not only a bad melody, but a distortion of truth, a debasement of the order of creation. And, obviously, bad music necessarily carries with it a note of moral evil. For music has an *ethos,* a moral note or qualification, as Plato understood so well. To expose oneself to bad music means to introduce into oneself a disorder fraught with consequences for the spiritual life. Hence, the passionate concern of those early Cistercians, that their music, like all other aspects of their life, should conform to the exigencies of the authentic. How they would have delighted in Paul Hindemith's description of the way we perceive music. He writes in part that when we listen to music, the sound passes through our auditory senses, and that we "co-create" or "re-create," so to speak, an interior image that corresponds to the exterior sounding phenomenon. The outward music is interiorized within us. The moral is obvious: we should be careful what we listen to, since, in a sense, we become to some degree what we hear. This is a point of view that not all moderns would agree with, but it is surely well worth our consideration.

St. Bernard was deeply concerned for the moral effects of music. In his Letter 398 addressed to Abbot Guy and the community of Montièramey, he expressed his ideas about what liturgical music should be about. The letter was written to accompany the proper Office written by Bernard and his colleagues for the principal patron of Montièramey, St. Victor. I pass over the wonderfully descriptive words of Bernard, that sacred music should be resplendent with truth, and should foster within us virtues such as humble-mindedness, devotion, and justice, and should bring about spiritual light and discipline for our sense-faculties. The melodies should be serious, but also attractive, though in no way smacking of the lascivious or rustic;

they have to be composed with real musicianship and art. But the most important thing Bernard has to say, I think, is summed up in his formula, *Sensum litterae non evacuet, sed fecundet:* The melody "should not obscure the meaning of the text, but should rather make it fruitful, make it fecund." This, I suggest, is one of the major functions of liturgical music: to make the word more life-giving, more fecund than it is in itself. This is true, I think, even when the composition is purely instrumental, without material words—but this is a separate, though related topic. Here my main point is that the modern composer of sacred music would do well to write in such a way that his music makes the text more fruitful.

St. Bernard and the monks of his monastery would have been fascinated by what modern philologists are saying about the etymology of the Hebrew term for "word." Consensus is by no means perfect; but I myself am particularly attracted by the theory which makes the same Hebrew root consonants *D-B-R* appear in the words for Temple sanctuary (*debhir*), for desert (*midbhar*), and for word (*dabhar*). Not all scholars agree that what binds these terms together is the basic meaning of *D-B-R,* as the preposition "behind". For myself, I like to think that there is indeed a link between the terms for "Holy of Holies" (*debhir*) and for "word" (*dabhar*). In either instance there is question of the divine presence and action behind the Temple veil, behind the word. God is *behind* the word, so to speak; and at any moment his presence and his action are liable to break through the shell of the word. We should remember that, in Hebrew, *dabhar* means both "word" and "event" or "happening." Wherever God's word is, then, God himself is present through that word—present and acting.

For the twelfth-century monk, the most important thing was to interiorize the sacred texts, to take them into one's deepest self. The twelfth century was still a largely an oral culture, so that memorization played an important role in the spiritual life. Memorization meant interiorization, so that words and music were stored away within the deep recesses of memory as a kind of silent music which, though sub-conscious, was still producing its effects. This might be an important consideration for us moderns, whose senses are constantly being bombarded from without. Perhaps you know Plato's account in his *Phaedrus* about the inventor of writing, Theuth, who tried to persuade the King of all Egypt that writing would make the Egyptians wiser and would improve their memories. Replied the King: "The fact is your invention of writing will produce forgetfulness in the souls of those who have learned it. They will not need to exercise their memories, being able to rely on what is written, calling things to mind *no longer from within themselves...*" In the twelfth century, however, the baneful effects of writing had not yet run their full course, so that monks and nuns were still chanting texts which they drew from within themselves rather than from a printed page. Does this have anything to say to us, with our muzak culture and our virtually total dependence on TV, radio, and CDs?

So far I have touched only tangentially on Boethius' profound concept of a *musica mundana,* a "music of the spheres." This music is the principle that brings order into the whole cosmos as it moves through space and time in its solemn, mysterious dance. We have to be in tune not only with our deepest self, but with the entire cosmos. The whole of monastic ascesis was aimed at reversing the disorder created by sin, so that the individual could once more fall into step, with the help of God's grace, and enter into the great sweeping rhythm of love and truth which forms the very essence of this *musica mundana,* this music of the spheres. For us moderns, it is probably more congenial to think of the music that we ourselves create as being rooted, if not in the music of the spheres, at least in a music that comes to us from above.

There are numerous stories from medieval monastic literature which take for granted a connection between our sacred music and the music of heaven. There was, for example the thoroughly disreputable lay brother from Clairvaux, who three times apostatized and three times was received back by St. Bernard. His third return was marked by a genuine change of heart; but it was also the beginning of a long and painful illness. As he lay dying, however, he received a momentary foretaste of the life to come. As the chronicler tells it (*Exordium Magnum* IV, xvi), he "straightway broke forth in a *jubilus* of high heaven's praise; and, with face calm and serene, this poor unlettered rustic, who had never learned how to chant or read, began to sing with melody of the sweetest from those new, ever delectable hymns and chants from the canticles of Zion." And the text goes on to speak of our "cantor" chanting even now, in death, the Alleluia which is being sung in the streets of the heavenly Jerusalem.

I think, too, of the vision of an illiterate monk by the name of Christian (*Exordium Magnum* I, xxxiv), who saw the community of Cîteaux gathered in choir and chanting the divine praises, while above them yet another choir—this time a choir of angels—was busily singing the same liturgy of praise. This clearly means that the brethren here below were already participating in the liturgy of heaven.

Which brings me to a very similar account from the 20th century. When the great French musicologist Nadia Boulanger lay in a coma just a few days before her death, Leonard Berstein came to visit her, despite that fact that any kind of communication was absolutely impossible. Suddenly she spoke: "Dear Lenny ..." He searched his mind anxiously for the right thing to say, and then heard himself asking: "Do you hear music in your head" Instant reply: "All the time." Bernstein continued: "And what are you hearing at the moment?" He thought of her preferred loves. Mozart? Monteverdi? Bach? Stravinsky? Ravel? Long pause. And then: "One music...with no beginning, no end." She was already there, wrote Bernstein, on the other side.

And this is the great challenge for the contemporary composer of sacred music: to write music that already anticipates and shares in that music from above; a music that has no beginning and no end; a music that draws us even now to the other side.

The greatest danger for the contemporary composer of sacred music is perhaps well expressed by the novelist Thomas Klise, who wrote in his book, *The Last Western,* "Now art glorifies the artist, affirming the part above the whole." In the twelfth century, sacred music was still being composed by anonymous composers. They wrote music that was often utterly ravishing, but also utterly gratuitous: something perfect done with love and supreme skill for love of God, and without any view to permanency. Far from glorifying the artist, their art glorified God and served the faithful, without calling undue attention to itself, and without losing sight of its humble place within the liturgy as a whole. The contemporary composer of sacred music deserves our sympathy. After all, he or she has to earn a living. These modern composers have to send their two or three kids through college; and this they can do only with an eye on royalties and on their established reputation as serious composers of sacred music. Still, we would do well to look back to earlier centuries as paradigmatic for contemporary practice.

We already have a tradition of plainsong and polyphony that can serve us well as a means of participating in the liturgy of heaven. But this in no way means restricting ourselves to the glories of Gregorian chant or renaissance polyphony. Fidelity to tradition, if this is genuine, always means a creative fidelity. The contemporary composer of sacred music in the aftermath of Vatican has incredible possibilities, but always in continuity with the best of tradition— which, after all, means the past living on in the present, and leading us into the future. Only let our contemporary sacred music be a sharing in that music from above, a music which is one, without beginning, without end.

Father Chrysogonus Waddell, O.S.C.O., has been a monk of the Cistercian Monastery of Gethsemani in Kentucky since 1950. He was ordained to the sacred priesthood in 1958. He studied liturgy and theology at St. Anselmo's in Rome, and has long been active in the areas of composition, monastic studies, and the liturgy.

V.

The Music of Cosmic Liturgy: How Benedict XVI's Vision for Sacred Music Might Sound in an American Parish

Susan Treacy

A constant theme of Pope Benedict XVI in his writings on liturgy and on music is that of "cosmic" liturgy, that is, liturgy as something that we do not create but participate in as a link between heaven and earth. But this transcendent liturgy also has an incarnational aspect that is firmly rooted in historical time and actual human culture. Mystery, too, is an attribute of the liturgy that, again, is not something that we initiate, but is all about the God who loved us first and who awaits our response.[1]

The Holy Father has more than once posited an inextricable connection between song and cosmic liturgy. As early as 1978, then Archbishop Joseph Ratzinger wrote of the cosmic character of the liturgy and its relationship to music. The Jews believed that the glory of God was only to be found in the Temple at Jerusalem, but at Christ's crucifixion, when the Temple veil was rent in two, the glory of God departed the Temple to dwell where Jesus now lives—in heaven and in His mystical body, the Church. So now songs of praise to God ring out both in heaven and on earth, filling the entire cosmos.[2] In his most recent essay on the subject of music and liturgy, to be found in the Holy Father's book entitled *The Spirit of the Liturgy,* Pope Benedict cites Psalm 57, where the psalmist, in speechless awe of God, bids his soul, his harp and his lyre to awaken the dawn. Together with "the peoples," they will sing of the magnificent glory of the Lord, the glory that at their summons will spread over the entire earth.[3]

Of special significance for Benedict XVI is that he was born on Holy Saturday and baptized at the Easter Vigil. In his memoirs he wrote: "To be the first person baptized with the new water was seen as a significant act of Providence. I have always been filled with thanksgiving for having had my life immersed in this way in the Easter mystery, since this could only be a sign of blessing."[4] The infant Joseph Ratzinger lived the first hours of his life in the context of cosmic worship, the uniting of heaven and earth through the solemn recounting of the history and the mystery of Redemption by Christ Our Passover. *Cantemus Domino*, the song of Moses in Exodus 15, is one of the canticles of the Easter Vigil, and in his writings the Holy Father has noted over and over again that this first description of liturgical singing in the Bible signifies the central event of Judaism, the deliverance from bondage in Egypt, about which Jewish parents were exhorted to remind their children never to forget.[5]

The redemption of the people of Israel was permanently realized, however, by the new, the true Exodus that Christ effected for His people, the new Israel. The Holy Father reminds us that this Song of Moses reappears in Revelation 15: 3, where it is now a song of victory sung by the saints, victorious against the "satanic trinity: consisting of the beast, its image and the number of its name."[6] But it is also the song of the Lamb, Christ Our Passover, sacrificed on the Cross and truly risen. Just as the Israelites sang their new song of liberation from Egypt, but still faced the years in the wilderness, so Christians sing the new song of Jesus while they face the "already but not yet" of unconsummated history, life punctuated with suffering that can be elevated through songs of praise to the Lord.

Many songs of praise—as well as songs of supplication, of lament, and of the whole range of human experience—can be found in the Psalter, Israel's hymnal, which became the hymnal of the New Israel, the Church. King David the Psalmist was now superseded by Christ the King, "the true David." The Fathers reinterpreted the Old Testament, including the Psalms, in light of the New Testament. *Now* the words of the psalms were imbued with Christological significance. Over time, as the Church established the *pericopes* for liturgical reading, and other liturgical texts, especially those of the Mass Propers, these texts became recognized as a Patristic commentary on the psalms. An examination of the *Graduale Romanum*, which contains all of the Proper chants, will reveal that most of their texts come from the Book of Psalms.

Many of the Holy Father's writings address the crisis—ongoing since Vatican II—in Catholic liturgical music. In *The Spirit of the Liturgy* the pope sums up his earlier ideas and assesses the current situation. He cites "three developments in recent music" that "epitomize the problems that the Church has to face when she is considering liturgical music."[7] The first problem is that of enculturation—how to reconcile in sacred music the universality of the Church with indigenous musical traditions. Here the Holy Father does not seem to propose a definitive solution; instead, he focuses more on the second and third developments. The second is that contemporary "classical" music "has maneuvered itself, with some exceptions, into an elitist ghetto, which only specialists may enter—and even they do so with what may sometimes be mixed feelings."[8] The destruction of tonality in the early twentieth century by Arnold Schoenberg and his disciples created a world of sound that was difficult for many people to embrace.[9] The third development is that because of the extreme dissonance and sterility of contemporary "classical" music by Schoenberg and others, popular music gained primacy in the hearts of most people. The pope, however, distinguishes between true popular music (of the *populus*) as opposed to the commercialized, "industrially produced" "pop" music, which "has to be described as a cult of the banal."[10]

For the liturgy, however, because it is truly cosmic, Pope Benedict writes that high art is "a necessary way of expressing belief in the world-filling glory of Jesus Christ. The Church's liturgy has a compelling mandate to reveal in resonant sound the glorification of God which lies hidden in the cosmos. This, then, is the liturgy's essence: to transpose the cosmos, to spiritualize it into the gesture of praise through song and thus to redeem it; to 'humanize' the world."[11] This is to be accomplished through sacred music that is *pars integrans in liturgia*[12] and is "holy," "true art," and "universal," to quote Pope Saint Pius X.[13] That music, Pope Benedict reiterates, is Gregorian chant, which literally *is* the sung liturgy, and sacred polyphony, both old and new.[14]

So…what *would* the music of cosmic liturgy sound like in an American parish? We would do well to follow the guidelines in the Holy See's *Musicam Sacram* and the *General Instruction on the Roman Missal*. *Musicam Sacram* indicates the primacy of singing not only for the faithful, or for the choir, but also for the priest and ministers. Article 5 of this 1967 Instruction on Music in the Liturgy reads:

> Liturgical worship is given a more noble form when it is celebrated in song, with the ministers of each degree fulfilling their ministry and the people participating in it. Indeed, through this form, prayer is expressed in a more attractive way, the mystery of the Liturgy, with its hierarchical and community nature, is more openly shown, the unity of hearts is more profoundly achieved by the union of voices, minds are more easily raised to heavenly things by the beauty of the sacred rites, and the whole celebration more clearly prefigures that heavenly Liturgy which is enacted in the holy city of Jerusalem.[15]

This last sentence also recognizes the idea of cosmic liturgy by making a reference to the heavenly liturgy described so vividly in the book of Revelation. As Pope Benedict has written: "When man comes into contact with God, mere speech is not enough. Areas of his existence are awakened that spontaneously turn into song."[16] *Musicam Sacram* then reiterates in a more direct way the Catholic Church's ideal of the completely sung Mass. Article 27 of the Instruction reads:

> For the celebration of the Eucharist with the people, especially on Sundays and feast days, a form of sung Mass (*Missa in cantu*) is to be preferred as much as possible, even several times on the same day.

Article 28 goes on to mention "different degrees of participation…put forward here for reasons of pastoral usefulness, so that it may become easier to make the celebration of Mass more beautiful by singing, according to the capabilities of each congregation." This is based on the 1958 Instruction of the Sacred Congregation of Rites, *De Musica Sacra*, Article 25, which offered a method gradually to introduce and increase active participation at Mass by the faithful through singing. The first degree of participation in *Musicam Sacram* includes the dialogues between the priest and people. In contrast to *De Musica Sacra*, the post-Vatican II document also includes the priest, whereas the earlier Instruction focused merely on getting the people to sing. This first degree of participation is so integral that it "may be used even by itself." The second and third degrees, however, may not be used without also using the first degree. The second degree includes, essentially, the Ordinary chants other than the *Sanctus*, which was considered to be an acclamation, and is thus assigned to the first degree. The Proper chants (and the hymns that are usually substituted for them) and the Scripture readings comprise the third degree of participation. How many parishes do you know that follow these degrees of participation? How can this situation be remedied?

For the Mass in English, Father Samuel Weber has been engaged in a great and worthy project to provide parishes and religious communities with English-texted chants in continuity with tradition. Father Samuel has set the English texts of the Mass Propers to simple chants, or chant-inspired melodies. Some of these you had an opportunity to sing already at this convention session and at today's Mass, a votive Mass of the Most Holy Eucharist.

At that Mass you also heard some of the traditional Gregorian chant Propers, sung in Latin, and some sacred polyphony. Thus, in my talk, my model will be that of a weekly celebration of the *Novus Ordo Missæ* in Latin. In the interest of time we shall listen only to selected portions of the Mass. I have chosen the 4th Sunday of Advent because I have examples of recorded chants from that Sunday which illustrate the three degrees of participation.

The Mass begins with the Introit, or Entrance Antiphon—*Rorate Cæli*—part of the third degree of participation, which would be last in the order of learning to sing the Mass. As important as the Propers are, and it *is* so beneficial to present the "mystery of the liturgical season or festivity,"[17] the Introit and other Proper chants are among the more ornate and difficult chants and are usually, though not always, sung by the choir or *schola.* In the words of this Introit we see an example of patristic Scriptural exegesis. The text of the antiphon, from Isaiah 45: 8 and Psalm 18: 1, refers to King Cyrus of Persia, God's chosen instrument to restore the Jews to their homeland after decades of captivity in Babylon. But the messianic character of the passage is made even clearer by its inclusion as the Introit text for the 4th Sunday of Advent. The antiphon is an entreaty to sky and earth to bring forth the Savior, but the verse—from Psalm 18—proclaims that God will perform this mighty deed. From the outset we are led into the mystery of this 4th Sunday of Advent; our Savior is on the way and anticipation quickens. Now the celebrant chants his salutation in the name of the Trinity. He need not sound like Pavarotti; in fact, it is better that he not, for such an individual quality of voice would call attention to itself rather than to the sacred liturgy.

Presumably, the dialogues of the Entrance Rites include, in addition to this greeting dialogue and the Collect, the Penitential Rite when it is in dialogue form, as it is in Option A, *Miserere nostri, Domine.* In Advent, a penitential season, the *Gloria* is not sung.

The next section I shall play for you includes the Offertory Antiphon *Ave Maria.* One of the most beautiful Gregorian chants, this includes the texts from the Gospel of Luke, the salutation of the angel Gabriel and the exclamation of Elizabeth at the Visitation of the Blessed Virgin.

The most cosmic part of Mass occurs during the beginning of the Eucharistic Prayer, with the Preface dialogue, followed by the Sanctus. In the dialogue that ensues, the celebrant bids the faithful "Lift up your hearts" to the Lord. The chant for the preface dialogue is among the most ancient recitation formulas in the repertory of Gregorian chant. The priest then continues with the Proper Preface for the 4th Sunday of Advent. In the *Sanctus* the faithful join with all the angels and archangels and heavenly powers in singing the praises of the thrice-holy God. On this recording the choir and congregation sing the *Sanctus* from Vatican Mass XVII, which is designated for Sundays in Advent and Lent.

So far you have not heard any sacred polyphony. Any of the Ordinary and Proper chants could be sung in polyphonic settings, so here is the Communion antiphon for the 4th Sunday of Advent, as set by William Byrd (1543-1623).[18] The text is the well-know passage from Isaiah 7:14: "Behold a Virgin shall conceive and bear a Son, and shall call His Name Emmanuel."

When all is said and done, it is the Mass itself that should be sung, not just songs at Mass.[19] Of course, the Mass in and of itself (i.e., without singing) is cosmic liturgy already, but as Pope Benedict points out, it is singing (and music in general) that imparts a truly cosmic dimension to the celebration of the Holy Sacrifice of the Mass.

The music of cosmic liturgy, especially Gregorian chant, is sublime yet humble. It is not meant to sound like Hollywood's impersonation of the heavenly choirs—two hundred high women's voices singing in three- or four-part harmonies, accompanied by a full symphony orchestra. It is merely the voices of the celebrant—the *alter Christus*—and the faithful, along with all of creation and the heavenly host, offering their sacrifice of praise, *una voce dicentes,* to the Lamb upon the throne.

Susan Treacy, Ph.D., is Professor of Sacred Music at Ave Maria University in Naples, Florida. She has also taught at Franciscan University of Steubenville, Luther College, Emory University, and the University of Oklahoma. She holds her doctorate in historical musicology from the University of North Texas; she also has an M. Mus. in opera from the Manhattan School of Music, as well as a B. Mus. in voice from the Oberlin College Conservatory of Music. Her research interests are in Catholic liturgical music and English devotional song. In addition to her scholarly articles, Dr. Treacy writes a regular column, *Musica Donum Dei*, for the *Saint Austin Review* (StAR). She also directs the Women's *Schola Gregoriana* at Ave Maria University, and formerly directed the *Schola Cantorum Franciscana* at the Franciscan University of Steubenville (where she was also a section leader and soloist with the Bach Choir of Pittsburgh). She served as a member of the editorial committee for the *Adoremus Hynmnal* and currently serves on the Board of the Church Music Association of America.

Endnotes

[1]Joseph Ratzinger, "Liturgy and Church Music," *Divini Cultus Studiorum: Studies in the Theology of Worship and of Its Music,* ed. Robert A. Skeris. *Musicæ sacræ meletemata*, Vol. 3 (Altötting: Verlag Alfred Coppenrath, 1990), pp. 190-191.

[2]Joseph Ratzinger, "Theological Problems of Church Music," *Crux et Cithara: Selected Essays on Liturgy and Sacred Music*, trans. and ed....by Robert A. Skeris. *Musicæ sacræ meletemata*, Vol. 2 (Altötting: Verlag Alfred Coppenrath, 1983), pp. 219-220. This essay was originally a lecture to the Church Music Department of the State Conservatory of Music at Stuttgart, it was first published with the title "Church Music, a Spiritual and Intellectual Discipline" (Stuttgart, 1978).

[3]Joseph Ratzinger, *The Spirit of the Liturgy* (San Francisco: Ignatius Press, 2000), p. 136.

[4]Joseph Ratzinger, *Milestones: Memoirs*, 1927-1977 (San Francisco, 1998), p. 8.

[5]Exodus 13: 3-9

[6]Ratzinger, *Spirit of the Liturgy,* p. 137.

[7]Ratzinger, *The Spirit of the Liturgy,* p. 147.

[8]*Ibid.*

[9]That hegemony, however, was challenged all along by composers such as Maurice Duruflé and Ralph Vaughan Williams, to mention just a few, and it has been destroyed by the more recent movements of neo-Romanticism and holy minimalism, represented by composers such as John Adams, Arvo Pärt, and Henryk Gorécki.

[10]Ratzinger, *The Spirit of the Liturgy,* pp. 147-148.

[11]Ratzinger, "Theological Problems of Church Music," p. 221.

[12]*Cf. Sacrosanctum Concilium*, Art. 112. Austin Flannery, O.P., ed., *Vatican Council II: The Conciliar and Post Conciliar Documents,* 1988 Rev. Ed. (Northport, NY: Costello Publishing Co., 1987), p. 31.

[13]Pius X, *Inter Sollecitudines,* Art. 2.

[14]Joseph Ratzinger, "Sing Artistically for God," *A New Song for the Lord: Faith in Christ and Liturgy Today* (New York: Crossroad, 1996), p. 105. Here Pope Benedict also includes "church hymns" along with Gregorian chant and sacred polyphony in the Church's musical patrimony.

[15]Austin Flannery, O.P., ed. *Vatican Council II: The Conciliar and Post Conciliar Documents,* 1988 Revised Edition (Northport, NY: Costello Publishing Co., 1987), p. 81.

[16]Ratzinger, *Spirit of the Liturgy,* p. 136.

[17]*General Instruction of the Roman Missal, Including Adptations for the Dioceses of the United States of America* (Washington, DC: United States Catholic Conference, Inc., 2003), Art. 47.

[18]From his *Gradualia*

[19]In *Documents on the Liturgy,* Section I. General Documents, DOL 508, is appended a footnote to Musicam Sacram, Art. 33.33. It is desirable that the assembly

of the faithful should participate in the songs of the Proper as much as possible, especially through simple responses and other suitable settings.The song after the lessons, be it in the form of gradual or responsorial psalm, has a special importance among the songs of the Proper. By its very nature, it forms part of the Liturgy, of the Word. It should be performed with all seated and listening to it—and, what is more, participating in it as far as possible. R4

R4   Query: Many have inquired whether the rule still applies that appears in the Instruction on Sacred Music and the Liturgy, 3 Sept. 1958, no. 33: "In low Masses religious songs of the people may be sung by the congregation, without prejudice, however, to the principle that they be entirely consistent with the particular parts of the Mass." Reply: That rule has been superseded. What must be sung is the Mass, its Ordinary and Proper, not "something," no matter how consistent, that is imposed on the Mass. Because the liturgical service is one, it has only one countenance, one motif, one voice, the voice of the Church. To continue to *replace the texts of the Mass being celebrated* with motets that are reverent and devout, yet out of keeping with the Mass of the day (for example, the *Lauda Sion* on a saint's feast) amounts to continuing an unacceptable ambiguity: it is to cheat the people. Liturgical song involves not mere melody but words, text, thought, and the sentiments that the poetry and music contain. Thus texts must be those of the Mass, not others, and singing means singing the Mass. *Notizie* 5 (1969), p. 406, quoted in Thomas C. O'Brien, ed. and trans., *Documents on the Liturgy, 1963-1979—Conciliar, Papal, and Curial Texts,/* International Commission on English in the Liturgy (Collegeville, MN: Liturgical Press, c1982), p. 1299.

The 4ᵗʰ Sunday of Advent

Introit

Isaiah 45:8; Psalm 18:1

(Entrance Antiphon)

RORATE CÆLI desuper, et nubes pluant iustum: aperiatur terra, et germinet Salvatorem.

Ps. Cæli enarrant gloriam Dei: et opera manuum eius annuntiat firmamentum. Rorate cæli…

SKIES, let the Just One come forth like the dew, let Him descend from the clouds like the rain. The earth will open up and give birth to our Saviour.
Ps. The heavens declare the glory of God, and the firmament proclaims the work of His hands. Skies…

Greeting
Act of Penitence
Kyrie eleison
No Gloria for Advent

Offertory

Luke 1: 28, 42

AVE MARIA, gratia plena, Dominus tecum: benedicta tu in mulieribus, et benedictus fructus ventris tui..

HAIL MARY, full of grace, the Lord is with thee. Blessed art thou amongst women, and blessed is the fruit of thy womb.

Luke 1: 28, 42

HAIL MARY, full of grace, the Lord is with thee. Blessed art thou amongst women, and blessed is the fruit of thy womb.

Advent Preface II

VERE dignum et iustum est; æquum et salutare, nos tibi semper et ubique gratias agere: Domine, sancta Pater, omnipotens æterne Deus: per Christum Dominum nostrum.

Quem prædixerunt cunctorum præconia prophetarum, Virgo Mater ineffabili dilectione sustinuit, Ioannes cecinit affuturum et adesse monstravit. Qui suæ nativitatis mysterium tribuit nos prævenire gaudentes, ut et in oratione pervigiles et in suis inveniat laudibus exsultantes.

Starting on December 17

FATHER, all-powerful and ever-living God, we do well always and everywhere to give you thanks through Jesus Christ Our Lord.
His future coming was proclaimed by all the prophets. The virgin mother bore Him in her womb with love beyond all telling. John the Baptist was His herald and made Him known when at last He came. In His love Christ has filled us with joy as we prepare to celebrate His birth, so that when He comes He may find us watching in prayer, our hearts filled with wonder and praise.

Et ideo cum Angelis et
Archangelis, cum Thronis et
Dominationibus, cumque omni
militia cælestis exercitus,
hymnum gloriæ tuæ canimus,
sine fine dicentes:
Sanctus, Sanctus, Sanctus…

And so, with all the choirs of angels
in heaven we proclaim Your glory and
join in their unending hymn of praise:
Holy, Holy, Holy.

Communion Antiphon
ECCE virgo concipiet, et pariet
filium: et vocabitur nomen eius
Emmanuel.

VI.

Session II
Opera Avtis – Domus Dei

Image As Sacrament: Rediscovering Liturgical Art

Denis R. McNamara

Among the many contentious points in the discussion about the sacred liturgy in the years since the Second Vatican Council is the place of imagery in churches. Most of us know of older churches whose statues were removed, either thrown away or relocated to some other place in the parish. We have heard about churches whose murals were pulled off the ceiling or painted over with the ubiquitous institutional cream-colored paint. But the truth of the matter is that if you look at some old pictures of churches, the riot of imagery evident was at times overwhelming, with an Infant of Prague next to the Sacred Heart next to a six-foot revival crucifix—all in the sanctuary which itself had murals behind the altar of Christ in the carpenter shop on one side and the Agony in the Garden on the other. Meanwhile, the tabernacle might have been a small cupboard buried deeply in a Gothic altarpiece. Even architect Ralph Adams Cram, one of the twentieth century's fiercest defenders of traditional architecture, famously described these overwrought Victorian sanctuaries in their "frantic elaboration looking, alas! Like a glorified soda fountain."[1]

But of course the answer to the dilemma of un-theological visual clutter is not the imageless, barren churches of concrete block and red clay tile found in the 1970s and 80s, or the lifeless oceans of cream-colored drywall of the 1990s. The answer to the dilemma is also not the willy-nilly purchase of catalogue statues inserted into a 70s, 80s or 90s church to make it "feel" churchy, though admittedly, that is often better than the alternative. The answer to the dilemma of imagery is to return to the foundational theology of the sacramental image, adequately categorizing different kinds of images, and use them properly. We must learn again what images are, or to use the language of Hans Urs von Balthasar, "we must return to the primary contemplation of what is *really* said, really presented to us, really meant"[2] by liturgical imagery. The lack of understanding of what images really are to the liturgy has led to artistic distortion and destruction.

So what I propose to do is divide this essay into four parts. The first part will introduce the basic theology of the image as sacrament, that is, the bearer of presence. The second makes distinctions between different kinds of images and how they are best to be used. The third categorizes the understanding the liturgical image in the 20th century and shows how a failure to understand images as sacramental lead to the various upheavals experienced in the last few decades. Lastly, it will look at some recent examples and make some recommendations for the current day.

The Theology of the Image

In his *Letter to Artists*, Pope John Paul II wrote that "in a sense, the icon is a sacrament. By analogy with what occurs in the sacraments, the icon makes present the mystery of the Incarnation in one or other of its aspects"(LA, 8). The word "icon" itself comes from the Greek word "to resemble," but is more than a merely factual similarity. The perfect icon is Christ, as image of the Father, who in the incarnation takes what was previously unknowable to the senses and gives it material form. By taking flesh from the Virgin, God consented to be made visible and tangible. His real, actual presence was mediated by matter, revealing that which was otherwise unknowable to the senses: "He who has seen me has seen the Father" (Jn 14:9). The heavenly and the earthly meet in Christ Jesus. In his *Apology for Divine Images*, St. John Damascene claimed that the incarnation of Christ provides the theological foundation for the making of liturgical images. Since Christ joined spirit and matter to make himself present to the world, so by analogy, sacred images follow suit making Christ present sacramentally in the medium of art.

Any truly iconic image of Christ in the western tradition, even if three dimensional, does not end in making a historical reconstruction of what the earthly face of Jesus of Nazareth, the earthly carpenter, looked like. The job of the liturgical image is to reveal both the divine nature and the human nature of Christ. It makes present the very reality that it signifies, which is why Pope John Paul could call it a sacrament. An iconic image represents in art the reversal of that chaos and loss of divine life which occurred in the Fall. It prefigures our hoped-for heavenly future and makes it knowable to the senses. This is why eastern theologians of icons speak so often of the "Taboric" light, the light which showed the transfigured Christ and revealed his dazzling, heavenly radiance on Mount Tabor. The job of a maker of liturgical images is to allow the Holy Spirit to use him or her to re-present, present again, the heavenly dimension of Christ, a saint, the Heavenly Jerusalem, or a new earth. When an image is truly sacramental, it presents a spiritual reality through the mediation of the earthly matter of which it is made.

Leonid Ouspensky's important work, *The Theology of the Icon*, gives specific guidance on the making of iconic images.[3] Whether made in Eastern manner as we think of the word "icon," or in a more western version, sacramental images always show a divinized humanity, not merely a fallen earthly body. For this reason, icons never represent a living person, one who has not yet experienced the fullness of heavenly glory, and the subject of icons are limited to canonized saints.

The iconic image reveals the holiness of the person portrayed, showing the glorious, eternal face of a divinized person participating in the divine life which consumes the earthly passions. Ouspensky put it this way:

> ...the icon is an image not only of a living but also of a deified prototype. It does not represent the corruptible flesh, destined for decomposition, but transfigured flesh, illuminated by grace, the flesh of the world to come...this is why grace, characteristic of the prototype, is present in the icon. In other words, it is the grace of the Holy Spirit which sustains the holiness of both the

> represented person and of his icon…The icon participates in
> the holiness of its prototype and, through the icon, we in turn
> participate in this holiness in our prayers.[4]

This understanding of the image is quite old, for as the Second Council of Nicaea (787) had decreed: "The more often we gaze on these images, the quicker we who behold them are led back to their prototypes in memory and in hope."[5]

Though iconic images represent a heavenly reality, it is a reality where grace has perfected nature, and the image will have earthly characteristics. Evidence of gender, age, and racial characteristics are often included, because for an image to be recognizable, the characteristic traits of a saint are to be preserved in a stable iconography. So St. Peter the Apostle is always shown with his keys, St. Therese with her roses, Maximilian Kolbe with his striped suit from Auschwitz. Even the Russian Orthodox St. Peter the Aleut, an Alaskan, is sometimes shown wearing his heavy, fur-lined winter coat, which is nonetheless portrayed as a divinized, unwrinkled, perfected winter coat.

So if the notion of a sacramental image is understood properly, it most obviously rules out some of the abuses seen here and there in recent years, like portraying images of Karl Rahner or Martin Luther King, Jr., in Catholic churches. I read recently about a new statue which was installed in a church which showed Saint Joseph wearing jeans and sneakers in order to help people in the parish think of him as more real and less remote. However, the result of this approach is to make St. Joseph seem less heavenly—and that is a serious theological error. It reminds me of a group of women religious whose vocation advertisement headline reads "less like saints and more like you." Religious life in a sense is about making an iconic life on earth, prefiguring the eschatological perfection of heaven by living as far as possible the heavenly life to come. With iconic religious imagery, the same principle applies.

In some cases, naturalism has been abandoned altogether in liturgical imagery, making art either so abstract or so distorted as to be nearly unrecognizable or even monstrous. This intentional distortion of religious art, common through the 1960s and 70s, grew from a reaction to the often saccharine and overly-pretty "holy card" art of the previous generations. Theologians like Paul Tillich, working on Lutheran presuppositions about the shattered nature of the human's *Imago Dei*, believed that sacred images could only be used if they represented the human condition of anxiety, guilt and despair. Tillich called this the "Protestant Principle" in art, where images would be distorted to express the ugliness of the fallen human condition itself rather than the anticipated perfection of heaven. Although this theology is foreign to the Catholic understanding of the liturgical image, it was nonetheless widely influential on Catholic art as early as the 1950s.

Interestingly, in reaction to the denial of naturalism and surface beauty in the art of recent decades, a new hyper-realism has sprung up in liturgical and devotional art. While this at first glance may seem an improvement, often these images present only the earthly reality of a saint. Of course one has to assume that people mean well when they make these decisions, but better decisions could have been made if a proper understanding of the sacramental image were part of the decision-making process.

Kind of Images

In my reading there are really three types of images for ecclesial use, and understanding these types can have great impact on the way our churches come to be embellished. I have categorized them into three groups: liturgical, devotional, and historical.

First, there are liturgical images. These sorts of images represent the heavenly liturgy itself as known from the vision of heaven given to Saint John in the Book of Revelation. John and an angel walk through the heavenly city with a golden measuring rod and notice that the Heavenly Jerusalem is composed of golden, gem-covered walls radiant with light. They also see the angels and saints praising God, dressed in vestments, offering bowls of incense at the throne of God and saying such phrases as "Holy, holy, holy, Lord God of hosts."

Saint John describes heaven like this:
There in heaven stood a throne, with one seated on the throne!
...around the throne is a rainbow that looks like an emerald.
Around the throne are...twenty-four elders dressed in white robes with golden crowns on their heads...around the throne...

are four living creatures, full of eyes in front and behind: the
first like a lion, the second like an ox, the third with a face like a
human face, and the fourth like a flying eagle (Rev 4: 2-5).
After these things I looked, and behold, a great multitude which
no one could number, of all nations, tribes, peoples, and tongues,
standing before the throne and before the Lamb, clothed with
white robes, with palm branches in their hands, and crying out
with a loud voice, saying, "Salvation belongs to our God who sits
on the throne, and to the Lamb!" All the angels stood around the
throne and the elders and the four living creatures, and fell on
their faces before the throne and worshipped God (Rev 7: 9-12).

Since this is the best we know of the heavenly liturgy,
it provides the basis for our liturgical texts. In the great Tradition,
this description became the basis for the Mass, as recently noted by
theologian Scott Hahn and others. Christian artists represented this
heavenly liturgy in churches as soon as they had the means, a tradition
which remained unbroken until the middle of the twentieth century.

Representing this heavenly scene in images makes art which
is fundamentally *liturgical*, showing the golden walls and angels and
saints of the heaven. Here the iconic arts makes present and active
the reality it signifies, sacramentally making present to us the setting
and communities of the heavenly liturgy which are not normally
knowable to our senses: the angels, the saints, the Trinity itself, and
the souls in purgatory. Since it is this heavenly liturgy into which we
enter sacramentally in the earthly liturgy, full, conscious and active
participation demands an encounter with the fullness of the liturgy,
including its heavenly and cosmic dimensions.

It is worth noting that this approach to liturgical imagery is
very different from placing a bunch of catalog-ordered devotional
statues around the sanctuary for people's private devotions, no matter
how pious this may at first appear. Liturgical images, whether grand or
modest, are a unified whole representing the heavenly liturgy. They are
fundamentally public and intimately intertwined with the solemn and
public prayer of the Church. Because at the time of the Second Vatican
Council liturgical art was often confused with devotional art, many
people felt free to denude Catholic churches, often rightly, claiming
that devotional items did not belong in the sanctuary surrounding the

altar. The unfortunate response at times, though, was to remove both liturgical and devotional images and leave nothing in their place.

The second category to be discussed is devotional imagery. This type of image serves for veneration which is fundamentally private and associated with individual piety, or might perhaps be associated with para-liturgical events. This might be a stand-alone image of the Sacred Heart, Our Lady of Lourdes, or St. Lucy with her eyes on a plate. These images are legitimate, wonderful and necessary to support the prayer life of the faithful for the same reason that devotions are: they flow from and return to the liturgy. But if one makes the appropriate distinctions, they are *not* primarily liturgical because they are not represented in the context of the liturgy of heaven or earth. The leaders of the 20th century liturgical movement rightly claimed that liturgical imagery belongs in its own place, such as a separate chapel or shrine rather than in competition with the altar and liturgical art of the sanctuary.

In the third place are images which are fundamentally historical. These images may include sacred history in subjects as lofty as the Christ child in the carpenter shop in Nazareth or the Wedding at Cana. But it might just as well include scenes like the conversion of Constantine, military victories, or the sisters and children next door in the school. These images are often didactic and honorary, and in the case of Biblical imagery, perhaps worthy of meditation, but they deal with topics less closely connected to the liturgy itself. Sometimes, however, the biblical imagery is from Christ's Passion, and it becomes more closely associated with the re-presentation of the Passion, which is deeply intertwined with the liturgy, and so the lines can indeed blur. Historical images have their rightful place, but their place is usually tertiary, behind liturgical and devotional.

Liturgical Imagery in the Twentieth Century

When thinking about liturgical decision-making, one soon sees that the Church and the Christian culture truly work on long cycles of decades and centuries. Many of the liturgical battles that we are having today are responses to decisions made in the 1970s, which were themselves responses to the decisions made in the 1890s, 1920s or 1940s. And as is often the case, the liturgical pendulum often swings too far to both sides before settling in the beautiful mean between excess and deficiency. Usually it is the more sensible reformers and the moderate language of ecumenical councils which get the ideas right.

Take for instance, the quotation from *Sacrosanctum Concilium* about imagery in churches. Section 125 reads:

> The practice of placing sacred images in churches so that they may be venerated by the faithful is to be maintained. Nevertheless their number should be moderate and their relative positions should reflect right order. For otherwise they may create confusion among the Christian people and foster devotion of doubtful orthodoxy.

This sounds quite serious. While retaining the use of images in the Church, the Fathers of the Council give a rather stern warning about creating confusion and doubtful orthodoxy. And the solution to this problem, they write, is keeping the number of images moderate and arranging them to reflect right order. Why would this be on the minds of the Council fathers?

Well, here is one answer. Let's look at a Victorian Gothic church in Killarney, Ireland. It certainly is the antithesis of the sterile boxes of the 1970s, but it also deserves some severe criticism. Every possible form and shape of ornamentation has been applied to wall, altar, cloth, and statuary. The large vine patterns on the wall are over-scaled, and, of course, the altar and tabernacle are nearly lost in all of this. The altar is somewhat buried under the reredos, so all that one can really see is half an altar rather than an entire altar. The tabernacle is a little cupboard built into the screen behind which is overshadowed by the multiple devotional images piled up around it. One could make the claim that this assemblage represents the glory of the heavenly assembly, but it is something of a chaotic mess of pieces not in right order and not moderate in number. This is the sort of thing that *Sacrosanctum Concilium* was seeking to correct.

The Convent Chapel of Dominican Sisters in Kentucky, from the mid 19th century, serves as another example. The image clearly shows how this is more about being "Gothic" with its crockets and finials than it is about being theological. Of course this high level of craft and effort certainly raises the status of the room, and there are some devotional images, but where is the heavenly liturgy? Another example is the now removed original interior of Saint Mary's Church in Lake Forest, Illinois, where scenes from the carpenter shop in Nazareth clearly overwhelm the relative scale and complexity of the altar.

These sorts of Victorian Churches received much criticism from architects even as early as the 19s and 20s, long before the radical iconoclasm of the post-conciliar years. The desire was not to rid churches of imagery, but to make it make sense theologically and liturgically. In 1923 Maurice Lavanoux, one of the founders of *Liturgical Arts* magazine, lamented that altars had become "vehicles for architectural virtuosity" rather than true liturgical assemblages.[6] One of the leading figures of the American Liturgical Movement, H. A. Reinhold, said that the 20th century reform of the liturgy could be summed up by saying that proper churches would put "first things first again, second things in the second place, and peripheral things on the periphery." This meant liturgical art would be primary, devotional art secondary, and everything else on the periphery.[7] It decidedly did not mean that empty churches denuded of imagery were the solution to the problem.

In the early years of the twentieth century, some artists really understood their liturgical theology, like the Cincinnati-born muralist, Felix B. Lieftuchter. His murals in the Cathedral of St. Joseph in Wheeling, West Virginia, show the sophisticated and deeply liturgical 20th century liturgical response to Victorian clutter. Certainly this artistic scheme is rich, figural, layered, complex, and for lack of a better word, "churchly." Here we see the heavenly liturgy, and this truly is liturgical art. Though it has been misunderstood for decades, this sort of imagery is of the essence of the liturgy itself. Looking at this sort of imagery, even during Mass, is indeed *not* a distraction, but in fact a visual participation in the heavenly dimensions of the liturgy. Christ, reigning in glory, is shown seated on a throne surrounded by angels, canonized saints and the white-robed multitudes, while the "river of the water of life," which the *Catechism of the Catholic Church* calls a symbol of the Holy Spirit, goes rushing forth from the heavenly city. The figures are legible, recognizable, western in their derivation, but also iconic, showing the glorious, divine quality of heaven. The starry sky above the heavenly city sits above the golden buildings in the background and the radiant divinized quality of the heavenly beings whose gaze is centered on Christ.

Another of Lieftuchter's great murals is in the Cathedral of the Madeleine in Salt Lake City, Utah. Though it shows a similar heavenly scene, rather than "the one seated on the throne," it presents the Trinity with Christ crucified. The Book of Revelation tells us that John sees Christ in many forms in heaven: crucified and risen, and as a lamb standing as though it had been slain. This mural emphasizes the sacrifice of Christ, but is decidedly not a historical scene from the Holy Land, nor is it a revival cross for devotion to the suffering Christ. Rather, it is a heavenly scene, where a glorified crucifixion represents the continuing and eternal sacrifice of Christ to Himself to the Father, without losing any sense of the sorrow of Christ's passion. Even the angels show a heavenly sorrow. The mural is clearly western in its representation but is nonetheless iconic because of its representation of the anticipated, divinized, nature of the heavenly realities.

There are other ways to represent this heavenly reality, however. In his famous St. Thomas Episcopal Church in New York City, architect Ralph Adams Cram used stone sculptures to represent the orderly array of heavenly beings that form part of the worshipping assembly. He modeled this great wall of sculpture on the medieval chapel at Merton College in Oxford. Again, these images are neither primarily devotional nor historical but *liturgical*. They make present to us the otherwise invisible heavenly participants in the liturgy. Since these beings are already present and active in the liturgy, making them knowable to the senses makes them sacramental images. At St. Luke's Church in Saint Paul, Minnesota, a similar arrangement was made on a smaller scale. Here a glorified crucifixion is surrounded by saints and angels who form part of the cloud of witnesses to the earthly liturgy. A similar scene is presented in mosaic at Transfiguration Church in Philadelphia, where heavenly beings ponder a glorified crucifixion—the eternal sacrifice.

In a late example, Cincinnati architect Edward Schulte, one of the great unsung twentieth-century Catholic church architects, used something of a modern idiom to represent the angels and saints of the heavenly liturgy. In his 1962 Church of Saints Faith, Hope and Charity in Winnetka, Illinois, the golden saints recognizable because of their symbolic attributes, are expressive of their heavenly state, free of the earthly passions. This is clearly iconic, liturgical art that is not a distraction from the liturgy. It *is* the liturgy. A favorite phrase of the liturgical movement was "don't sing at Mass, sing the Mass," encouraging people to sing the words of the Mass itself like the *Kyrie* and the *Gloria* rather than devotional hymns. Instead of being satisfied with devotional images alone, we can say "look at the Mass" in all of its many dimensions as represented in properly liturgical art. The heavenly liturgy is to be known by the eyes as well as the ears.

Because much of the sacramental theology of the liturgy was forgotten, it should come as no surprise that liturgical art and architecture itself would no longer be thought sacramental. Already in nineteenth-century architecture, which many people hold up today as an ideal of liturgical richness, the distinction between liturgical art and devotional art was widely lost. The piling up of devotional art, which crowded out the altar and tabernacle, truly proved an artistic challenge to the primacy of the altar and tabernacle. All throughout the early decades of the twentieth century, loyal, traditional, Catholic architects were arguing that there had to be something better and that it had to grow from the nature of the liturgy itself. "Move the devotional art away from the altar," they said, "and replace it with liturgical art." And for a short while they did. Then other ideas came to the fore.

Many bad concepts about liturgical imagery of the 1960s and 1970s were based on truths only half understood. Ideas about simplifying churches were exaggerated to justify the removal of all art from a sanctuary or even an entire church. Distortions in the idea of what the worshipping "assembly" meant lead to thinking that the liturgy was limited to an earthly, domestic, corporate community meal—one which had no place for devotional or heavenly realities. The distortions concerning what active participation means are too many and too deep to go into here, but it is certainly clear that the leading scholars of the twentieth-century liturgical movement saw active participation in the liturgy as the forming of a Mystical Body with Christ as its Head which offered itself as a victim to the Father. This body entered into the mysteries through the rites of the Church in order to glorify God and share in the divine life by seeing heavenly things, singing heavenly texts in a heavenly manner, making appropriate and ordered heavenly gestures, and eating and drinking the heavenly food of the heavenly Wedding Feast of the Lamb in the sacramental species of the Eucharist. When this understanding of the liturgy was lost, there was no longer perceived to be a need for the liturgical image.

Because many churches had used devotional art in the sanctuary instead of liturgical art properly understood, many architects and liturgical consultants were justified in doing some spring cleaning. However, many architects and liturgical consultants had no idea that there *was* a distinction between liturgical and devotional art, thinking that every image was devotional, and therefore not germane to the liturgy. So out they went. And newly-built churches often did not get any imagery at all unless it was an image of the Blessed Virgin Mary in a corner. And the People of God were left with empty barns and meeting halls.

I hope to end by looking at some recent pieces of church art, many of which were award winners and runners up in the liturgical design awards given by liturgy magazines, the editors of which appear to me to have little understanding of how sacramental theology impacts the design of liturgical art. One example shows the Holy Family apparently dancing in a circle, hands joined, and with big smiles. This dancing Holy Family has its good points in that it is legible, recognizable, full of joy, and perhaps causes the viewer to reconsider the earthly life of the child Jesus Christ. It goes without saying, however, that this sort of image falls into the category of historical art, and then only of the most speculative kind. I would be quite surprised to find someone lighting candles or kneeling in front of it for devotional purposes because it is self-enclosed, self-referential, entirely earthbound, and encourages spectatorship rather than participation.

Another much celebrated image is the Marian shrine at the Catholic Chapel of Saint Ignatius at Seattle University. The Marian shrine is so abstracted as to reduce the Blessed Virgin Mary to a bowl of milk flowing over a rock. A contemporary news article accompanying the picture reads: "The piece is meant to suggest elements such as 'source,' represented by the bowl, 'flow' represented by the streaming milk, and 'figure' represented in the way the stone sculpture is shaped in the traditional outlines of Marian shrines." So the artist tells us that it is source, flow and figure, not the woman prepared at the beginning of time to be Theotokos, conceived without original sin, the New Eve, the Queen of the Apostles, Queen of the Most Holy Rosary, and so on. In fact, she is not even recognizably human. The result is what the artist intended it to be. Although the average person is often intimidated by the famous artist who supposedly has some secret knowledge of art, there is no mystery here. The image does not look like the Blessed Virgin because it was never intended to. As theologian Father Edward Oakes, S. J., says, "Art doesn't lie." It may not express the Truth, but it always tells you what its maker intended it to be. By contrast, one can discuss the image of the Virgin over the door of the new Los Angeles Cathedral. The hyperrealism of the image, a nicely-executed sculpture of the fashion model next door, binds it too closely to the earthly realm. While its naturalism makes it legible, its lack of abstraction, and therefore universality, makes it narrow and merely human.

Aside from the overly abstract and the overly realistic, there is also the image which is simply absurd. As an example, I offer the infamous statue of St. Thomas Aquinas at the Catholic parish at the University of Virginia in Charlottesville, which is made of reclaimed chrome-plated car-bumpers. The image is so dominated by the obvious novelty of making a statue out of car bumpers that the material cannot become a bearer of the heavenly and allow the sacramental to burst forth. Rather than being a participation in the heavenly reality of the divinized glory of Saint Thomas Aquinas, which then becomes a bearer of grace to us through the Holy Spirit, it becomes an unusual art piece with a historical subject rather than a sacramental or devotional image.

To finish up, I will propose a phrase that I have developed to help guide artists. In addition to being complete and theologically accurate, liturgical art must be *naturalistic enough to be legible, abstracted enough to be universal, and idealized enough to be eschatological.* Its naturalism will make art a perceptible sign to the human senses, yet a proper abstraction will find the universal out of the many examples, and preventing it from being overwhelmed by earthly details. This universality is the first step toward an idealization which allows that a liturgical image might radiate with eschatological anticipation of our perfected heavenly future promised by Jesus Christ. These ideas are at the heart of the Eastern understanding of the icon, and the West could use this approach to "breathe with both lungs' in the field of liturgical art. This approach, which sees liturgical art not as a distraction from the liturgy, but as integral to the worshipper's eye as a Scripture reading to the worshipper's ear, would at the very least warm up our empty churches and make them feel welcoming and inviting. But more importantly, it would make a building "look like a church" not out of sentimental emotional attachment to old ways, but because the church building will become the sacramental manifestation of the *Church* in all of its natural and supernatural components. This is why *Sacrosanctum Concilium* 123 asks that liturgical art and architecture reveal the "signs and symbols of heavenly realities." When the heavenly realities are manifested sacramentally, a church will look like a church because it will by definition be a church, and the sacramental, liturgical image plays a central role in successful church design.

Dr. Denis McNamara is Assistant Director and faculty member at the Liturgical Institute of the University of St. Mary of the Lake/ Mundelein Seminary in the Archdiocese of Chicago, where he teaches courses on culture, aesthetics, and liturgical art and architecture. He holds a BA in the History of Art from Yale University and an MA and PhD in Architectural History from the University of Virginia in Charlottesville. He has authored articles in *Communio, Homiletic and Pastoral Review, Rite, The Priest,* and *Sacred Architecture.* His recent book, *Heavenly City: The Architectural Tradition of Catholic Chicago* (2005), was recently granted a Benjamin Franklin Award from the Independent Book Publishers' Association. He also serves as a liturgical design consultant.

Endnotes

[1]Ralph Adams Cram, *The Gothic Quest* (New York: Baker and Taylor, 1907), 240.

[2]Hans Urs von Balthasar, *Glory of the Lord,* Vol. 1: *Seeing the Form* (San Francisco: Ignatius Press/Crossroads, 1983), 32.

[3]Leonid Ouspensky, *The Theology of the Icon* (Crestwood, NY: St. Vladimir's Seminary Press, 1978), particularly Chapter Ten entitled "The Meaning and Content of the Icon."

[4]Ouspensky, 191.

[5]Council of Nicaea II, cited in the "Order for the Blessing of Images for Public Veneration by the Faithful," Book of Blessings, Chapter 36, footnote 27.

[6]Maurice Lavanoux, "An Architect's Dilemma," *Orate Fratres,* 3 (14 July 1929), 278-79).

[7]H. A. Reinhold, "The Liturgical Church," *Church Property Administration* 5 (June-July 1941), 8.

VII

Domus Dei et Domus Ecclesiae: The Church Building as a Sacred Place

Duncan Stroik

It is common to describe architecture as having three characteristics: *Firmitas*, *Utilitas,* and *Venustas.* These are the ancient principles of Durability, Convenience, and Beauty, which make clear the importance of durable construction, the ennoblement of function, and visual beauty in the definition of architecture. These three principles apply to all architecture, including the architecture of the church building. Other principles, such as harmony, symmetry, proportion, scale, and composition are necessary as well. In fact, it is possible to start with the triad *firmitas, utilitas,* and *venustas,* and arrive at the great variety of principles of architecture which architects and their patrons have promoted throughout time. This is to point out what might seem obvious, that no three principles, or five concepts, or a single text can explicate the multiplicity of principles required for good architecture to take place. The temptation to make simplistic explanations for architecture is age-old, and one that we have been guilty of falling into in recent years.

Liturgy and Architecture

Many Catholics believe the adage that the study of liturgy should inform the design of churches, as well as the reverse; that the architecture of our churches informs the liturgy. The idea that

the understanding of liturgy (or theology) is necessary to design a Catholic church has been foundational for church architecture since Vatican II, and has even spawned a new type of expert, the Liturgical Design Consultant or LDC. This new role seems to be based on the view that architects do not understand the liturgy and its architectural implications. Therefore, it is believed that the parish needs to hire a consultant who has expertise in this area and can design the "liturgical elements" of the church and can give direction to the architect. In spite of the fact that few LDCs have degrees in architecture, they often determine the choice of the architect and then tell him how he can or cannot design the church. But, we might ask, how could architects in the past have designed churches without a liturgical design consultant? Historically, the pastor, the bishop, or the patron was expected to be knowledgeable about liturgy and its architectural ramifications. Likewise, the architect was expected to know the tradition of Catholic architecture. For this to become the norm once again, it is necessary (following conciliar documents and canon law) that seminaries train future priests in liturgy and the history of Catholic art and that architecture schools expose students to church design.

Conventional wisdom suggests that if we would understand the liturgy and its requirements, then we would have buildings more appropriately designed for their purpose, resulting in an improved church architecture as well as an improved liturgy. The implication is that in previous (and less enlightened) eras, buildings were erected which were not suited for the liturgy. Is this really accurate? It is probable that many of the theologians, saints, and martyrs of the past millennium would be surprised to learn that the churches in which they worshiped undermined their active participation. If we look back at the church architecture of the past thirty-five years, presumably informed by the liturgy, one wonders what went wrong.

Of course, the view that architecture is first and foremost liturgical is not really an idea that originates with the Second Vatican Council. At the beginning of the twentieth century, many architects and church leaders believed that understanding both liturgy and theology was necessary for improving the design of churches. The ecclesiastical architecture movement in America, with its embrace of traditional architecture; and the Liturgical Movement in Germany, with its embrace of Modernism, were both concerned with how liturgical issues pertained to architecture.

When we compare a church designed by the modernist Rudolf Schwarz with churches designed by Ralph Adams Cram—built about the same time—we realize the variety of architecture produced by those interested in the liturgy. However, it should be noted that one difficulty with focusing solely on the liturgy as determinant of design is that it leaves out many of the other aspects of church building. Ironically, the writings of traditional architects and liturgists such as Cram, Webber, Comes, Roulin, and O'Connell

may have inadvertently set the stage for the development of a liturgical functionalism after the Second Vatican Council. The average church building built since 1960 reflects this functionalism.

Church Documents in Stone

Perhaps the most important difference between architects such as Maginnis and Walsh, designers of the National Shrine of the Immaculate Conception, who employed traditional languages in the first half of the twentieth century, and architects such as Pietro Belluschi, designer of the San Francisco Cathedral, who worked within the Modernist idiom in the second half of the century, is that the former understood liturgical implications in the light of the history of

architecture. Examples from architectural history were seen as the equivalent of Church documents in stone and necessary for study and analysis. While it is certainly helpful to seek to understand Church architecture from first principles, it is also crucial that eighteen hundred years of Catholic architecture be brought to bear on that understanding. Thus, it is crucial that any new documents on art and architecture treat architectural history in a competent fashion. And it is not enough to advocate a single "golden age" of Church architecture, whether it be early Christianity or the Medieval era, which is a type of "archeologism." A more Catholic approach to understanding the church building will consider all types of architecture, including the Gothic, Renaissance, Baroque, Neo-Classical and Neo-Gothic—styles which are beloved by the laity but are often excoriated by the experts.

The appreciation and study of the architecture of the past can help us to interpret or even develop the concepts of architecture relevant for Catholic churches. It can also provide a broader context in which to analyze contemporary wisdom about the design of churches. When we consider the broad tradition of architecture, a number of questions relevant to contemporary architecture come up:

- How many examples of centralized churches have altars in the center? Almost none before the Italian Renaissance, and most of those were quickly removed and replaced with high altars in a defined apse like sanctuary.
- Where in history do we find churches with interior proportions which are horizontal rather than vertical? Almost never. Even the Mendicant and Spanish Mission churches had some sense of verticality and length rather than horizontality and proximity.
- When was the theater type or fan shape ever employed as a building for the liturgy? Never, until the advent of Modernist architecture in the mid-twentieth century.

I believe some of these questions may lead us to conclude that much of what passes for architecture inspired by the Vatican Council has no bibliography, and no foundation in the history of Catholic architecture. It seems that much of the architecture of the past fifty years is partially a result of cultural amnesia, and of our willingness to accept every novel form as "legitimate innovation."

Concepts of the Church

How we conceive of the church building is crucial to how we
design and construct it. The first chapter of *Built of Living Stones* pro-
poses to define the church building theologically, but it does not go far
enough. I would like to offer six categories to help in conceptualizing
the church building, bearing in mind that all of these, as well as others, are necessary for understanding and designing churches. If one

tries to accommodate all of these ideas in the design of a church, the result will more likely be a successful project rather than being merely a "one-liner" without substance.

Six Definitions of a Church Building

1. The church is *liturgical*—it is a building which provides appropriate and ennobling places for the liturgical rites.
2. The church is *sacramental*—it is a building set aside for the reception of the sacraments.
3. The church is a *home* for the liturgical elements—the altar, ambo, baptistery, and tabernacle.
4. The church is *devotional*—it is a place for public and private prayer.
5. The church is *iconographic* and *symbolic*—it incorporates imagery which inspires us and teaches us about the lives of the saints and salvation history.
6. The church is *sacred*—it is a holy place in which we come in contact with the divine.

The Church as a Sacred Place

As an architect and a teacher, I am engaged daily with the exigencies of budgets, building codes, and worrying how to keep water out of a building. However, I believe that the crucial issue in Church architecture today is the development of the theological understanding of the "church as a sacred place." There has been very little written on this subject in recent decades, except perhaps to dismiss it. We can, however, find this concept of the sacred stated explicitly earlier in this century, and implicitly before then. Nonetheless, where the concept is stated most clearly is in the material evidence: the art and architecture produced by our forbears.

Perhaps one reason little was said about the theology of the church building in *Sacrosanctum Concilium* is that the Fathers of Vatican II did not perceive it was in need of correction at the time (SC 124). To conceive of the church first of all in theological terms—before getting into the requirements for the liturgy, the limitations of the budget, space, or the specific language or character of the building—allows us to see the big picture. These requirements are certainly important issues in the design of a church, but if we get sidetracked by them, we are often left with a compromised building.

Canon law states that "the term church signifies a *sacred building* destined for divine worship" (C.I.C. 1214). In a certain way, the "church as a sacred place" can be seen as an overarching concept of architecture. Thus, liturgy and devotion can both be seen as taking place within the sacred place. This concept is understood as encompassing the related concepts of *domus Dei, domus Ecclesiae*, temple of the Lord, heavenly banquet, and the New Jerusalem.

Church as *Domus Dei*

A Spanish style cathedral in Chile or an onion-domed church in Russia may look worlds apart, but both buildings clearly look like churches to most people. Within the rubric of the "church as a sacred place," I am particularly intrigued by the concept of *domus Dei*, since it puts the focus on the object of our worship, and it originally was the

title of the American bishops' document on architecture. I searched in vain to find any reference to the concept of the church as the house of God within the document. This was a significant weakness of the draft. However, the bishops' discussion of architecture came at an opportune time, because we have gone on building without this concept for too long, and an emphasis on the church as a *domus Dei*, as well as on its other theological names, can have a most salutary affect.

House of God and Gate of Heaven

Hans Memling painted a wonderful image entitled "The Gate of Paradise" which shows the portals of a Gothic cathedral with angels standing in niches, on pinnacles and entering the church. It is a

wonderful interpretation of the meaning of the church building inspired by a famous story from the Old Testament. In Genesis 28: 10-17, we read that the patriarch Jacob, while journeying through Canaan, lay down in a certain place to sleep, and saw in his dreams a ladder to heaven on which angels were ascending and descending. In response, Jacob announces "How awesome is this place! This is none other than the house of God, and this is the gate of heaven." (Gen 28:17). *Haec est Domus Dei et Porta Coeli.* Throughout the ages Christians have called their churches *Domus Dei* and *Porta Coeli.* This name describes a dwelling and the One whom we seek to meet therein. It describes a building constructed for the purpose of coming into God's presence, and which must be worthy of its owner. And while we acknowledge that God cannot be contained in a building, we also know that He has chosen to make Himself known to people in sacred places from the earliest times.

House of God vs. House of the Church

The terms *domus Dei*, or house of God, and *domus Ecclesia*, or house of the Church, have both had a long history of use. Some modern commentators have sought to pit these two concepts against one another as if the church building must be either one or the other rather than "both/and." Their argument goes something like this: originally the house churches where Christians gathered were termed *domus Ecclesiae* (house of the Church) and only later was its name corrupted into the title *domus Dei* (house of God). This new title of *domus Dei* resulted in the overly sacral architecture of the Early Christian, Gothic, and Renaissance periods. Rather than seeing these

terms as mutually exclusive, I would prefer to see the concept of *domus Ecclesiae* as complementary to the concept *domus Dei*, allowing us to have a fuller understanding of a building which is a house for God and for his people. It is also tenable to see the idea of *domus Ecclesia* residing within the *domus Dei* (and visa versa). The house of the Church is by definition also the house of the body of Christ, and therefore the house of Jesus Christ the head.

Icon of Eternal Realities

Terms such as "sacred place," *domus Dei* and *domus Ecclesiae* help us to understand that the church building is more than the sum of its parts. Church architecture is not only a response to liturgy and to methods of construction, but more importantly it is an icon of eternal realities, that is, a window into spiritual reality, which Catholics understand to be more real than our life in this "vale of tears." Most of these titles for the church building are time-honored and have a basis in scripture or tradition. In recovering these concepts, it is essential to explicate them through the use of examples from various times and places. Ultimately, how we define the church building will affect how it is designed, how much money is expended, and to what kind of architectural standards it is constructed. Is your parish church a Temple of the Lord or a Worship Center? Is it an Assembly Hall or the Gate of Heaven?

The Church as Heavenly Banquet

It is interesting to recall the description the Russian envoys sent back to Prince Vladimir of Kiev when they visited the church of Hagia Sophia in Constantinoble: "We knew not whether we were in heaven or on earth. For on earth there is no such splendor or such beauty, and we are at a loss how to describe it. We only know that God dwells there among men, and their service is fairer than the ceremonies of other nations. For we cannot forget that beauty." Based on this visit, so the story goes, Russia chose to join with the Orthodox rather than with the Church of Rome.

Temple of the Lord and City on a Hill

Another term for the church is "temple of the Lord." It describes a holy place, a place of worship and adoration, a building where we are in awe, where we kneel before our maker, and where priests prostrate themselves on the floor during Good Friday. Just as the Jewish Temple, the church is seen as the place of sacrifice. The church as a "city on a hill," or "New Jerusalem," refers to the location of our churches on a

high place, with the sense of being a fortified and a protected sanctuary. In Europe, many towns, monasteries and religious shrines are built on the heights. In America, many of our religious houses, seminaries, and colleges were also built in this manner.

In proposing these names, it is important to point out that the concepts they embody are universal and applicable to different periods and styles. This universality is made evident when we compare the interior of the early Christian church of Santa Sabina in Rome—built in 425—with Brunelleschi's church of S. Lorenzo, built 1000 years later in Florence at the beginning of the Renaissance. 500 years after Brunelleschi's death, at the height of the industrial age, the parish of St. Andrew in Pasadena, California, built a wonderful basilica which refers to San Lorenzo and Santa Sabina. This is because the basilica

type and the meanings it embodies are timeless and as relevant today as in previous ages. In art and architecture great ideas have a long life. In order to recover a full understanding of Catholic architecture today, we need to re-appropriate as many of these time honored concepts as possible.

New Church Architecture

If we are building a "worship environment" or "liturgical space," it is much easier to get away with building a prefabricated shed, carpeting the floor, and using industrial materials, since it is conceived essentially as a functional structure. This is because we are conceiving of the church in the most narrow and mundane terms. You get what you pay for, but you also get what you ask for. If we tell the parishioners and the architect that it is the house of God and the house of the Body of Christ that we are building, then a banal structure will be much more difficult to sell. This is because people's expectations will be higher, translating into a higher quality design and greater generosity on the part of the parishioners.

If we begin with a rich theological understanding of the church as a "sacred place," we are more likely to build churches which are examples of *Firmitas*, *Utilitas*, and *Venustas*. Liturgical and functional requirements should be accommodated, but will not necessarily determine the overall image of the building. Iconography, including devotional art, will not take away or distract us from participation in the liturgy, because statues and paintings will be ordered in such a way to be in keeping with the church as an image of the eternal. The church building will no longer be designed as a monovalent structure, but will be multi-layered. No longer will the contemporary concerns of liturgy vs. devotion, priest vs. laity, active participation vs. private prayer worry us, because the building will be a *domus Dei*, a house of God which can accommodate all of these conceptions and all people under one roof. Then once again, we can say with Prince Vladimir's envoys, King Solomon, and Jacob, "This is truly the House of God and the Gate of Heaven."

Duncan Stroik, of the Notre Dame School of Architecture, is a noted architectural educator and practitioner. He helped form and implement the new curriculum in classical architecture at the University of Notre Dame. His involvement in the new renaissance of sacred architecture led to the formation of the Institute for Sacred Architecture and the *Sacred Architecture* journal, of which he is the editor. In addition to publishing and lecturing, Stroik has organized conferences on sacred architecture, has led seminars in Italy, and has also been featured on television programs. He has designed houses in New England, Chicago, and Ireland; and churches in California, Nebraska, Arizona, and Kentucky. He has also designed civic buildings. He is presently engaged in ecclesiastical projects in Wisconsin, Texas, Indiana, and California, along with a commercial building in Milwaukee and a monastery in Chicago.

VIII

Session III
Liturgiam Authenticam –
Translation Matters

The Languages of
Liturgical Translation

Rev. Paul Mankowski, S. J.

The beginning of the Holy Gospel according to John:

> Before the origin of this world existed the LOGOS—who was
> then with the Supreme God—and was himself a divine person.
> He existed with the supreme Being, before the foundation of the
> earth was laid: For this most eminent personage did the Deity
> solely employ in the foundation of this world, and of every
> thing. This exalted spirit assumed human life—and from this
> incarnation the most pure and sacred emanations of light were
> derived to illuminate mankind: This light shot its beams into
> a benighted world—and conquered and dispelled that gloomy
> darkness, in which it was enveloped. To usher this divine
> personage into the world, and to prepare men for his reception,
> God previously commissioned and sent John the Baptist. This
> prophet came to give public notice that a glorious light would
> shortly appear—to excite all the Jews to credit and receive
> this great messenger of God. John himself openly disavowed
> all pretensions to this exalted character—declaring, that *he*
> was only appointed of God to give public information of this
> illustrious personage.

The "Gospel," very approximately, of the Lord. You have just
heard a reading from Edward Harwood's New Testament of 1768, or,

to give its full Harwoodian title: *A Liberal Translation of the New Testament; being An Attempt to translate the Sacred Writings with the same Freedom, Spirit, and Elegance, With which other English Translations from the Greek Classics have lately been executed, with select Notes, Critical and Explanatory.* The unadorned prose of the Bible, plainly, was not to Harwood's taste. Being a child of his age, he preferred marble to granite for every purpose. Listen to his rendering of the Lord's Prayer (fromMatthew 6:9-11):

> O thou great governor and parent of universal nature, who manifestest thy glory to the blessed inhabitants of heaven—may all thy rational creatures in all the parts of thy boundless dominion be happy in the knowledge of thy existence and providence, and celebrate thy perfections in a manner most worthy of thy nature and perfective of their own!

You get the point. Harwood wanted prose that could take a polish, and the New Testament just wasn't marmoreal enough, whence he was obliged to provide improvements and corrections in those places where the unsteady hand of the sacred author had blundered. As a critic, Harwood makes common cause with the present Bishop of Erie, Donald Trautman, who recently objected to the literal translation of the words *praeclarum calicem* in the First Eucharistic Prayer: "'Precious chalice', said Trautman, "when I hear those words, I think of a gold vessel with diamonds on it. Did Jesus, at the Last Supper, use a precious chalice or a cup? The gospels clearly say 'cup,' but even in the lectionary from Rome we have the word 'chalice' imposed on the inspired text to carry out this 'sacred language.'"

It is important to understand that, concretely, Trautman's taste is diametrically contrary to Harwood's at every point: where Harwood was shocked at the rusticity of the bible, Trautman is shocked that the Roman Canon is not biblical enough. Yet both men are so confident of the superiority of their taste that they see it, and not the text, as the translator's touchstone. Each would translate what he *wished* the original author had written.

"Translations are so much more enjoyable than originals," Ephraim Speiser laconically observes in his introduction to the Anchor Bible Book of *Genesis*, "because they contain many things that the originals leave out." The history of biblical translation knows its share of Harwoods, eager to remedy perceived defects by creative interpretation; but more interesting is the case of those striving to include everything that God put in the sacred text and to add nothing that he didn't: for the study of biblical renderings shows that each choice for fidelity in one dimension of transmission involves a sacrifice of fidelity in another. Apart from ideologized *targums* or the work of gross incompetents, every attempt at translating the Bible involves a series of compromises or trade-offs in which that which is transmitted intact from the original to the translations is achieved at a cost: namely, the cost of diminished accuracy in some other aspect. We might say, adapting Herbert Butterfield's quip about the term realism, "fidelity is not a coherent strategy of translation, but a boast."

In the latter half of the 20th century, for example, it was considered appropriate to translate the Bible not word-for-word but thought-for-thought: to forego formal for dynamic equivalence, as the jargon has it. No one has made a stronger case for this than Ronald Knox, in his work *On Englishing the Bible*. Said Knox:

> Words are not coins, dead things whose value can be mathematically computed...Words are living things, full of shades of meaning, full of associations, and, what is more, they are apt to change their significance from one generation to the next. The [biblical] translator who understands his job feels, constantly, like Alice in Wonderland trying to play croquet with flamingoes for mallets and hedgehogs for balls; words are forever eluding his grasp.

Knox was dead set against what he called "token words"—i.e., a single English word consistently used to convey a given word of your original. Suppose, he suggested, a translation committee faced with the text of Virgil decides to render the word *pius* by "dutiful." The translator "very soon realizes," he says, "that *pius* takes on a different shade of meaning with each fresh context. Now it is 'Aeneas, that dutiful son', now it is Aeneas, that admirable host', now it is Aeneas, that trained liturgiologist'." The same context-conditioned meanings will be found with biblical words. "If," Knox continues, "you set out to give [Latin] *salus* the meaning of 'salvation' all through the New Testament, you find yourself up against St. Paul inviting the ship's company during the storm to take a little food for the sake of their salvation."

"To use such a token-word," Knox argues, "is to abrogate your duty as a translator.Your duty as a translator is to think up the right expression, though it may have to be a paraphrase, which will give the reader the exact shade of meaning *here* and *here* and *here*."

Now this is a very strong argument, and if the Bible were a work on the order of Virgil's—from the fist of one man, completed on a single afternoon, self-standing and self-ratifying—I think it would be unanswerable. But, in fact, the Bible is a collection of books, written in three languages by numerous human authors over the course of a millennium and a half, not connected one with another by any intrinsic design but assembled on dogmatic grounds by the Church. That means the Bible translator may well have a different set of responsibilities than the man envisaged by Ronald Knox. Consider two graduate students: one studying classics, given 50 lines of the *Aeneid* to translate; the second, studying Hebrew grammar, given 50 lines that turn out to come from Isaiah. Both would accomplish their job by following Knox's strictures. But if the same 50 lines given the Hebrew student are to be rendered for use in a Biblical translation, the task and its attendant responsibilities are markedly different. Many words and expressions in Isaiah have a pre-history (in earlier parts of the Old Testament), and others have a life of their own in later parts of the OT and NT as well. Translating in the Knox manner according to passage context will obliterate these inter-textual connections, while token translation will illuminate them. Further, a Biblical text is not so much read as it is heard, not so much heard as re-heard, often hundreds of times in a single lifetime. It does not have to make us catch our breath, and the translator doesn't necessarily fail us by failing to rivet our attention on first hearing. Again, the Bible is a liturgical book, and its use in the liturgy means the translator has aids to understanding which the translators of Virgil do not, while he also has duties to preserve to the extent possible the meanings or imagery on which the liturgy has focused. Finally, there is a tradition of doctrinal interpretation, embracing not only the original text but its earlier translations, to which the Biblical translator must be accountable. While the Hebrew graduate student is perfectly justified in rendering Hebrew *ha'almah* by "young woman," in Isaiah 7:14, the man translating the Bible must be aware of the LXX translation *parthenos en gastri hexei* and the Vulgate's *virgo concipiet*, and of the unanimous doctrinal tradition that sees in this passage a prophecy of the virgin birth. So it is important to appreciate that there are significant gains in intelligibility made by the thought-for-thought or Dynamic Equivalence approach, and there are significant costs as well.

And it seems to be the case that those costs have begun to impress biblicists in recent years, and that the pendulum is swinging the other way. The success of Robert Alter's recent translation of the Pentateuch, called *The First Five Books of Moses*, has done much to vindicate the much maligned token words, for Alter makes it a point to preserve the token wherever possible. In his introduction, Alter deplores an expedient to which Dynamic Equivalence is prone, which he calls the Heresy of Explanation. As Digby Anderson expounds it:

> When accurate translation produces a word or phrase that the translators feel is strange or "inaccessible" to modern readers they adjust it so that it explains itself. The result is "a betrayal" and, since strangeness is a quality of the Hebrew original, the translation places "readers at a grotesque distance from the distinctive literary experience of the Bible in its original language." The sort of thing Alter has in mind in speaking of the heresy of explanation is the rendering of metaphors of body parts such as "hand" by the function for which they stand, e.g., power, control, responsibility. The substitution is needless—the meaning was clear anyway—and it subverts the literary integrity of the story in which it occurs where "hand" is repeatedly used in a connected way.

This Heresy of Explanation is nowhere more rampant than in the New American Bible (NAB) and the Revised New American Bible (RNAB), where, e.g., Mary's "for I know not man" becomes "for I have not had relations with a man." Matthew 19:12 gets the same makeover. The traditional token-treatment in the Revised Standard Version (RSV) is this:

> For there are eunuchs who have been so from birth, and there are eunuchs who have been made eunuchs by men, and there are eunuchs who have made themselves eunuchs for the sake of the kingdom of heaven.

And here is the RNAB version, in which we are spoon-fed the following exegesis:

> Some are incapable of marriage because they were born so; some, because they were made so by others; some, because they have renounced marriage for the sake of the Kingdom of heaven.

I don't deny that the passage is hard to understand or that the RNAB's paraphrase is edifying, but it is impossible to recover the word "eunuch" from the RNAB's explanation—or explanations, more accurately, since being incapable of marriage is not the same as having renounced it—quite apart from the fact that marriage is not the activity of which eunuchs are incapable.

There is another problem with the Heresy of Explanation beyond the distancing of the reader from the text and the loss of the verbal connections when the metaphor is decrypted: namely, the translator who locks himself into an explanation locks himself into an interpretation, even where that is a risky business. Take the common word for "seed"—Hebrew *zera*, Greek *sperma*— that often falls victim frequently to the explanatory impulse. Its metaphorical meaning of offspring, descendants, etc., is almost always recoverable from the token "seed" itself, which makes decoding unnecessary. But sometimes it's not even prudent. Consider 1 John 3:9. The King James Version gives: "Whosoever is born of God doth not commit sin; for his seed remaineth in him: and he cannot sin, because he is born of God."

Now there are several problems of interpretation in this verse, the thorniest of which is what is meant by *sperma autou*, "his" that is, God's—"seed." One can understand the desire to ride out ahead of the text here, since there is no direct apprehension of the phrase "God's seed" that is not heretical or grotesque. The RSV, while ordinarily conservative and cautious, renders it "God's *nature* abides in him," which would seem to affront the hypostatic union; the New Living Translation gives us "God's *life*," and the Contemporary English Version goes for broke with "God's life-giving power lives in them and makes them his children."

Five remarks about these explanatory translations: 1) they are not the same; 2) while each may be said to be lucid, the lucidity leads to theologically problematic misunderstandings, and each requires a *further* explanation to avoid heresy; 3) Biblical Greek had words for nature, life, and power, none of which the sacred author chose to employ; 4) the notion of God's seed would have been as difficult for the original audience of John's letter as it is to us; and 5) if the original phrasing, "his seed," were preserved in translation, the reader or homilist would be at liberty to follow his own lights in recapturing its meaning, whereas the explanatory translation cuts him off from other possibilities. What's the point then, of a gain in lucidity, if the translation becomes *more* lucid than the original text permits?

There's a certain amount of chicanery, on the part of the translator, in suggesting that the intelligibility he puts in the translation reflects an intelligibility found in the original text. C.S. Lewis found the underlying theological problem already vexing 16th century Catholic and Protestant controversialists.

> All parties were agreed that the Bible was the oracles of God. But if so, are we entitled to worry out the sense of apparently meaningless passages, as we would do in translating Thucydides? The real sense may be beyond our mortal capacity. Any concession to what we think the human author "must have meant" may be "restraining the Holy Ghost to our phantasie."

The problem may be broadened yet further, since the fact is that in several places the Bible is awkward, or ugly, or ungrammatical, or—as was suggested—flatly incomprehensible. Should its awkwardness, ugliness, grammatical solecism and incomprehensibility be reflected in the translation? I am aware of no translation, ancient or modern, that does not iron out at least some of the rough spots, either by way of way of conscious tinkering or as a consequence of the translator's control of his own grammar and diction. More fundamentally, I propose, the translator's approach will be guided by his own understanding—or lack of understanding—of the Bible as the *Church's* book, addressed in response to the Church's purposes.

Take a homely example, that of the Hebrew vulgarism *maštîn bqîr*. It occurs seven times in the OT, always in the connection of mass slaughter of male citizenry. Douay and the KJV intrepidly give the literal rendering "any that pisseth against a wall." All modern translations, by contrast, launder the expression as "males," making use of an explanatory paraphrase. But the Hebrew phrase was *deliberately* unseemly; it was intended to depict an ugly act by an ugly expression. Does the duty of fidelity require conservation of ugliness? Well, the Bible is the Church's book; so it can be argued both ways.

A more politically charged problem is the translation of 1 Cor 6:9f: "Do not be deceived. Neither neither fornicators, nor idolaters, nor adulterers, nor *malakoi*, nor *arsenokoitai*...will inherit the kingdom of God." The late Yale scholar John Boswell denied it, but it's beyond dispute that both terms refer to homosexual mischief, and as a consequence they have come under intense scrutiny. The difficulty is perhaps more pastoral than linguistic, as delicacy is here the enemy of accuracy. The first word literally means "soft," but the RNAB is almost certainly right to understand it to mean "boy prostitutes." The second, *arsenokoitai*, is a coinage of Hellenistic Judaism reflecting the LXX of Leviticus 20:13: those who lie with males. The translation "homosexual," confusing as it does appetite and activity, obviously misses the mark. For my money, the most accurate rendering is that of 1560 Geneva Bible, "neither wantons nor bouggerers," but even that requires a gloss on "wantons."

Or again, almost all of the NT, and some of the Old, was written in a language that was not the author's mother tongue, with the consequence that literary beauties are rare and, very frequently, the syntax is hopelessly snarled. The second sentence in Paul's Letter to the Ephesians contains 160 words in Greek. Almost no translator has the stomach to give us the English equivalent—as Ronald Knox says, "nothing...is so subtly disconcerting to the modern reader as having his intellectual food cut up into unsuitable lengths"—yet it can be argued that turning clumsy Greek into snappy English for aesthetic purposes is a kind of infidelity—*traduttore, traditore*.

And what of the beauties of the Bible? It is a sad irony that translators are easily able to reproduce the ugliness of their originals, and only very rarely able to reproduce the beauties. An Ecclesiastical Committee may decide that a beautiful translation is desirable, but you can't order verbal felicities the way you order olives on a pizza—the Muses don't come running at the snap of one's fingers. (I would maintain, by the way, that the ability to make beautiful prose translations from ancient languages is one of the most stingily endowed of all artistic talents.) Then too, the 16th century translators Coverdale and Cranmer (who were endowed with that gift) had almost too much natural music in their prose. In his famous Cambridge lecture on the Name and Nature of Poetry, A.E. Housman spoke of the way the supervenient beauties of poetry had physiological effects on his person:

> One of these symptoms [of poetry, says Housman] was described in connexion with another object by Eliphaz the Temanite, "A spirit passed before my face, the hair of my flesh stood up." Experience has taught me, when I am shaving of a morning, to keep watch over my thoughts, because, if a line of poetry strays into my memory, my skin bristles so that the razor refuses to act.

Moreover, Housman found himself thus put upon by Coverdale's psalter:

> As for the seventh verse of the forty-ninth Psalm in the Book of Common Prayer, "But no man may deliver his brother, nor make agreement unto God for him," that is to me poetry so moving that I can hardly keep my voice steady in reading it. And that this is the effect of language I can ascertain by experiment: the same thought in the Bible version, "None of them can by any means redeem his brother, nor give to God a ransom for him," I can read without emotion.

So the question presents itself: was the poetry Housman found in Psalm 49:7 poetry the psalmist put there and which Coverdale conveyed, or was it absent in the Hebrew and simply the gratuitous effect of Coverdale's melodious prose? I confess this verse does not transport me in its Hebrew original, but this may result from my own obtuseness in the matter. Yet the point is rather: where the original is drab, is beauty in the translation a betrayal? Does it make the hearer of God's word a dilettante where he would have a disciple, or does it compensate for the deficiencies of our own culture by making the text more memorable, and thus an object of contemplation? The question in our own time is moot, since various considerations have made it certain that, of all the hazards presented by biblical translation, a dangerous excess of beauty is not one of them.

I began my remarks with a quotation from Edward Harwood's rewriting of the NT as an example of translation as conscious correction of its original. Harwood's foppishness had no lasting effect—indeed, as far as I can tell, no effect whatsoever. A far more serious threat to fidelity has arisen in our time in the form of so-called Inclusive Language—a threat, in fact, to the very possibility of biblical translation. The feminist ideology behind IL explicitly regards the authors of the biblical text as suspect, and it explicitly views language itself with suspicion. It thus brings a moral fervor to a wide-ranging project of ideologically informed correction in which both the message of the original text and the vocabulary by which it is to be transmitted are subject to planned manipulation. Though it serves as a *pretext* for political emendation, the activity of translation itself is of no intrinsic value to proponents of IL.

In this company, it is not necessary to expatiate on the harms visited upon the Bible by IL. But we can illustrate the problem by looking at analogous attempts to right injustices by dislocating one part of the language, i.e., the Receptor Language, of translation.

Some years ago an Indian Jesuit told me that he was part of a team that translated the Bible into Tamil. He explained that Tamil has honorific and non-honorific forms of address, and that in the common spoken language males are addressed by means of the honorific and females by the non-honorific. He said that, in order that the Bible might be a political tool for cultural change, viz., acknowledgment of the equality of women, the translation team decided that the honorific form of address would be used for all persons in the Bible, regardless of sex. The only exceptions, he went on to mention, were Satan and Judas, who were assigned the non-honorific.

I trust you can spot the problem. By withholding the honorific forms of address from some characters and not others, one is implicitly conceding the derogatory semantic value—and extra-linguistic appropriateness—of the non-honorific form. But you have thereby created a private world in which the reader must decode your own value judgments—which are not those of the biblical authors—from your own encryption. Yet why stop at Judas and Satan? Why do Manasses and Simon Magus and Jezebel escape the treatment? The fact is that, once you have declared the common language untrustworthy and taken it upon yourselves to improve it, you can never, for any reason, put down your responsibility. Thus, once you have decided that it is immoral to use certain constructions of your mother tongue earlier understood to be innocent and depart from that tongue in translation, the whole work comes under moral scrutiny whether you wish it to or not.

The impact of morally motivated translation was made, indirectly but wittily, by William Laughton Lorimer in his brilliant 1985 rendering of the NT into Scots dialect: a good-natured exercise in Scottish nationalism as well as a minor masterpiece of philological scholarship. In his alternative version of Matthew, Chapter 4, on the temptation of Jesus in the wilderness, Lorimer exploits the potencies of moral evaluation latent in his patriotic project:

> Syne Jesus wis led awà bu the Spírit tae the muirs for tae be tempit bi the Deil.
> Whan he hed taen nae mait for fortie days an fortie nichts an wis fell hungrisome, the Temper cam til him an said, "If you are the Son of God, tell these stones to turn into loaves."
> Jesus answert, "It says i the Buik:
>> Man sanna líve on breid alane,
>> but on ilka wurd at comes
>> furth o God's mouth."

We all get the point. But if Lorimer was tongue-in-cheek, the IL proponents are in dead earnest. And yet this very earnestness demolishes their only tool of communication. This is evident even in the "compromise" biblical translations that boast of limiting themselves to "horizontal" IL. Once the translator eliminates the unmarked generic to a perceptible extent, he paradoxically puts exaggerated and misapplied emphasis on the maleness of the masculine forms that remain: in effect, all masculines become marked for gender.

For example, Father John Rock pointed out to me that the NRSV is generally ruthless in excising English "man" for Greek *anthropos,* but retains it in Romans 5—not unreasonably, when one considers the problems with the alternatives. But when we read in the NRSV, "sin came into the world through one *man,*" our confusion is genuine; precisely to the extent that our expectations are based on the NRSV grammar (without generic "man"), we will understand St. Paul to be speaking about one *male.* In introducing exactly the kind of misunderstanding for which they are invoked as the cure, the inclusive devices cut their own throat. And this is only to be expected. For the Bible is the Church's book. And once you find the Church untrustworthy, you may at points agree with her, but you can never let yourself be taught by her. Whence every time you suspect the Church has God wrong, your own position wins by walk-over. A Pyrrhic victory.

In conclusion, let me ask: has it ever occurred to you how coy God is with respect to His *ipsissima verba*? At all events, it seems we were not meant to mistake the shell for the kernel by worshipping God's utterance instead of Himself. Jesus spoke in Aramaic, yet apart from half-a-dozen transliterated vocables, we have nothing. The OT goes out of its way to teach us we're not getting God's mind mainlined. In Genesis 11, we are told that all the earth had the same words and pronounced them the same way. Then God, coming down to destroy the pretensions of the builders of the Tower of Babel, confused their language—all language, no exception being made for Hebrew. This means that, on the Bible's own terms, Hebrew is itself a corrupt language—and not, e.g., the language God spoke to Adam and Eve in the Garden. We were not given a Qur'an or a Book of Mormon containing unmediated divine utterances. As George Macdonald wrote, God saw to it that the letter, as it could not give life, should not be invested with the power to kill.

In taking as my title, "The Languages (pl.) of Biblical Translation," I hoped to show that both source languages and receptor languages are multiple, that there will never be a final definitive translation, that every choice for fidelity by one manner of speaking comes at the cost of fidelity elsewhere, and that, by viewing the Bible as the Church's book, created for her purposes and subject to her judgments, we might arrive at the humility to receive God's word, not as a political platform, but as she who received it as a person.

Father Paul Mankowski, S.J., teaches Biblical Hebrew at the Pontifical Biblical Institute in Rome, and is a Visiting Professor of Biblical Theology at the John Paul II Institute for Marriage and the Family in Melbourne, Australia. He has also taught at the Weston School of Theology in Massachusetts, and was an Assistant Professor of Classics and Philosophy at Xavier University in Cincinnati, Ohio. His articles and reviews have appeared in numerous journals, including *The Thomist, First Things, Touchstone,* and *Voices.*

Father Mankowski is a native of Indiana. He holds a BA in Classics and Philosophy from the University of Chicago, an MA in Classics and Philosophy from Oxford University, a Licentiate in the Old Testament from the Weston School of Theology, and a PhD in Semitic Philology from Harvard University. He was ordained a priest of the Society of Jesus in 1987. He is the author of *Akkadian Loanwords in Biblical Hebrew* (for which the movie rights are still available).

IX.

Learning How to Do Liturgical Translations

Kenneth D. Whitehead

I.

Vatican Council II's Constitution on the Sacred Liturgy, *Sacrosanctum Concilium*, is quite often quoted in order to remind people that the Council actually said that "the use of the Latin language, with due respect to particular law, is to be preserved in the Latin rites" (SC 36 § 1). There are those who wonder how and why, if Latin was indeed to be "preserved," we now have the vernacular liturgy virtually everywhere.

Actually, *Sacrosanctum Concilium* speaks about the retention of Latin in two other places besides the one just quoted. "Care must be taken," the document further specifies, "to insure that the faithful may also be able to say or sing together in Latin the parts of the Mass which pertain to them" (SC 54). Again, "in accordance with the age-old tradition of the Latin rite, the Latin language is to be retained in the divine office" (SC 101 § 1).

All of these supposed requirements of the Council concerning Latin in the liturgy, as everybody knows, are close to being a dead letter today, and have been for a long time. Although Latin survives in the liturgy to some small extent, its survival, such as it is, remains both rare and precarious.

What happened? Close readers of the Council documents have sometimes noticed that in the very next paragraph immediately following the one stipulating that Latin is to be preserved, *Sacrosanctum Concilium* goes on to say that "since the use of the vernacular, whether in the Mass, the administration of the sacraments, or in other parts of the liturgy, may frequently be of great advantage to the people, a wider use may frequently be made of it [the vernacular], especially in readings, directives, and in some prayers and chants" (SC 36 § 2).

The decision as to "whether and to what extent the vernacular is to be used" was given by the Council, significantly, "to the competent territorial ecclesiastical authority," that is, to the bishops, subject to confirmation "by the Apostolic See" (SC 36 § 3).

In other words, while declaring that Latin was to be preserved, the Council turned right around and authorized the vernacular as well; and, moreover, it placed the basic decision as to whether Latin or the vernacular would be used essentially in the hands of the bishops (with the permission of the Holy See). Each of the paragraphs just quoted from *Sacrosanctum Concilium* providing for the retention of Latin, in fact, was immediately followed by a qualifier providing that the bishops' conferences could, in effect, opt for the vernacular instead (see SC 54, and SC 101§1 and 2).

Thus, what happened, almost before the Council was over, was a massive and virtually universal rush on the part of the various bishops' conferences of the world seeking permission from Rome to go over to the vernacular. The Roman authorities at the time, apparently, saw little choice except to bend before the wind. By 1971, as Father Austin Flannery, O.P., documents in his summary of the question in his *Vatican Council II: The Conciliar and Post-conciliar Documents* (p.39), "the use of the vernacular in public Masses was left entirely to the judgments of episcopal conferences, to the judgment of individual priests for private Masses, and of the ordinary for the divine office in private, in common, or in choir."

How did it come about that Latin could be dropped so quickly and so thoroughly, especially in the face of the apparently quite definite Vatican II language that it was to be retained? Actually, as most historians of the Council record, sentiment in favor of a vernacular liturgy was running quite strongly, and was growing, from the very beginning of the Council. There were some 800 missionary bishops present at the Council who were mostly in favor of it and lobbied for it. The hierarchies in some countries such as in France and Germany were said to be planning to adopt the vernacular liturgy regardless of what the Council might decree about it. Numerous Council Fathers spoke openly against retaining Latin and some even objected that the Council proceedings were themselves being conducted in Latin. The vernacular Mass, in the view of many, was turning out to be one of those famous "ideas whose time has come."

Many of the bishops also proved to be less than proficient in the language, were often unable to follow the conciliar proceedings with understanding, and were especially hampered in the give-and-take of conciliar debate. Ironically, this helped the well educated but mostly progressive prelates from countries bordering the Rhine to dominate the Council proceedings to the extent that they did; they themselves knew Latin well even while they favored the vernacular.

It was not that this viewpoint was unanimous, however. Many Council Fathers, including Cardinal Spellman from New York and Cardinal McIntyre from Los Angeles, spoke up passionately in conciliar interventions in favor of Latin (Cardinal Cushing from Boston, by contrast, unsuccessfully tried to persuade John XXIII to let him pay for a simultaneous translation system for the Council).

Following the Council, the First Instruction on the Proper Implementation of the Constitution on the Sacred Liturgy, *Inter Oecumenici*, dated September 26, 1964, in some of its language, seems to assume the Latin will be carried on (see esp. IO 57 & 89). Most of the bishops and cardinals in the Roman Curia, in fact, were also said to be in favor of Latin, as was Blessed Pope John XXIII himself. Like many of the Churchmen of his generation, he was quite proficient in Latin, loved the ancient language, and constantly sprinkled his speeches and writings with Latin words and phrases. On February 22, 1962, eight months before the opening of the Council, John XXIII issued an apostolic constitution on the study of Latin, *Veterum Sapientia*, with the declared aim of preserving Latin in the Western Church.

His directives in this document were perhaps uncharacteristically stringent for this large-hearted pontiff: he strictly forbade Churchmen from publicly speaking or writing against Latin (a prohibition that ceased to be operative on the Council floor virtually as soon as the Council opened). The jovial pontiff, very strict in this directive, went on to require that seminarians be given "a sufficiently lengthy course in Latin" before beginning their study of philosophy and theology. He stipulated that Latin should be restored to the curriculum in Catholic institutions, and required that the major sacred sciences should be taught in Latin using Latin textbooks. He decreed that a syllabus for the teaching of Latin should be prepared for use throughout the Church, and that a Latin academy was to be established in Rome to carry out and promote all these requirements.

If the continued use of Latin in the Church could have been preserved by issuing directives to that effect, *Veterum Sapientia* should have qualified as such a directive and should have sufficed. In fact, it became a dead letter even more quickly than Vatican II's own stipulation that Latin should be preserved in the Church. It became one of the first in the long series of Roman rulings that, in the post-conciliar era, were simply disregarded.

In retrospect, Vatican II's language concerning the retention and preservation of the Latin must be seen as carefully balanced statements designed to secure the approval for the Constitution on the Sacred Liturgy both from those bishops who favored Latin and those who favored the vernacular. What quickly became clear in the post-conciliar era was that the great majority of the world's bishops belonged to the latter group favoring the vernacular. For better or for worse, the vernacular liturgy was brought in and now, after some forty years, is apparently here to stay.

II.

Once the basic decision to go with the vernacular liturgy was confirmed by the Holy See's general approval of the requests from the various bishops' conferences around the world, a whole new set of questions then inevitably arose relating to liturgical translations. The task of translating all of the Church's liturgical and sacramental books was immense; it was a huge, daunting task. It was not clear to anyone at the time how it was to be done.

Meetings among the bishops from the English-speaking world soon resulted in the formation of an International Commission on

English in the Liturgy (ICEL). ICEL was organized as an independent corporation governed by an episcopal board consisting of bishop-representatives from eleven English-speaking countries. Associate members came from a number of other countries where English was spoken. ICEL was to be responsible for producing the texts of the Church's liturgy in English.

Because of the nature and quality of the translations it produced, however, ICEL soon became a rather controversial body in its own right. From the very outset, many of the faithful found the new English liturgy somewhat less than inspired. The ICEL translators may have been aiming at the "noble simplicity" desired by *Sacrosanctum Concilium*, but the result they produced all too often turned out to be flat, pedestrian, and prosaic.

More than that, ICEL often seemed oddly given over to a certain kind of what can only be called *mistranslation*. Even Catholics who were not Latinists had to wonder why *et cum spiritu tuo* ("and with thy spirit") came to be rendered "and also with you"; or why the *Credo* ("I believe") we profess on Sundays and holy days was translated as "we believe"; or why the once very familiar *mea culpa, mea culpa, mea maxima culpa* ("through my fault, through my fault, through my most grievous fault") mostly just got dropped from the new English version of what had been known as the *Confiteor* ("I confess...").

I will not go into any more examples of ICEL mistranslations. We have been living with the English liturgy crafted by this body for around forty years now, and I have to assume that you already know what I am talking about and can even give examples of inadequate renderings if not actual mistranslations in the English liturgy. The question is: why? Why did the ICEL translators feel free to alter and even omit plain and simple Latin words in the way that they so often did? What does seem clear is that they did feel free to do this, and they in fact did do it. They simply do not seem to have felt bound by the Latin text.

When we seriously inquire why this should have been the case, and try to delve more deeply into the matter, we discover that, virtually from the time the Roman liturgy first began to be translated into English, the ICEL translators were following a free translation method called for in a little-known document produced by the "Consilium" which Pope Paul VI had appointed to manage the reform of the liturgy mandated by *Sacrosanctum Concilium*. Pope Paul VI's Consilium issued this document in 1969. Known as *Comme le Prévoit* from its French original, this document advocates what it calls a method of "dynamic equivalence" in translations. By definition, this means that translations do not need to be literal. According to this method, words and concepts in the original Latin can thus be replaced with terms deemed more relevant today by the translator. Adaptations supposedly suited to the spirit of the times can be freely adopted.

For example, "sacral language" is considered by some to be no longer necessary or appropriate in the modern world. Unfortunately, this viewpoint seems not only to have been shared by the ICEL translators, but also to have been the viewpoint of the authors of *Comme le Prévoit* itself. At one point the document asserts that:

> Many of the phrases of approach to the Almighty were originally adapted from forms of address to the sovereign in the courts of Byzantium and Rome. It is necessary to study how far an attempt should be made to offer equivalents in modern English for such words as *quaesumus* ["we beseech"], *dignare* ["to be considered worthy"], *clementissime* ["most merciful"], *maiestas* [majesty], and the like (13).

In point of fact, such honorific words are sedulously avoided in the ICEL English liturgy, although they remain very much a part of the original Latin text of the Roman liturgy. Presumably such words no longer accord with the modern democratic spirit, although why they are apparently no longer thought to apply to Almighty God is not clear (only later, perhaps, would it begin to dawn on people that the ICEL translators were quite consistent in what was apparently ideological principle that it was the "community" henceforth that needed to be stressed rather than Almighty God).

But all along, though, it turns out that the typical ICEL translations have been produced in accordance with a conscious theory that, even apart from literal accuracy—also excluded by the same theory—was almost bound to rob them of some of the grandeur, mystery, and dignity that ought to be required in any genuine liturgical text directed towards "the worship of the divine majesty" (SC 33). This was consistently true of many of the ICEL translations for the Mass and the other sacraments hurriedly done in the late 1960s and early 1970s and pressed into service in and around our altars throughout the English-speaking world. While we had no choice but to learn to live with these translations—they represented what the translation commission established by the English-speaking bishops produced—that did not mean that they could not have been better, much better.

III.

It was bad enough that the "first generation" of liturgical translations into English were not only done hastily; they were done in accordance with a defective theory of translation. We might have thought that the Church could do better with a "second generation" of translations. When the time came for a new set of liturgical translations, or retranslations, however, instead of improving with experience, the liturgical translation situation actually began to get worse.

This occurred at least in part because the ICEL translators, influenced like practically everybody else in our society by the rise of the modern organized radical feminist movement, became convinced that liturgical translations henceforth not only had to be "free" and non-literal and non-sacral; they also had to employ feminist so-called "inclusive language." Not only would liturgical texts henceforth be translated in accordance with the method of so-called dynamic equivalence, they would also be translated in accordance with modern feminist ideas of acceptable language.

I do not intend to go into great detail here about what radical feminist "inclusive language" is and what it does—essentially the radical feminists contend that the generic use of "man," as in the sentence, "man is born to trouble as the sparks fly upward" (Job 5:7), does not include women, and hence special language must be devised that does include them, regardless of how the meaning and structure standard English may be distorted in the process.

But I am not going to get into the many examples of this that could be cited. Not all of them are as bad as the New Revised Standard Version Bible's "Follow me and I will make you fish for *people*" (Mk

1:17) for "fishers of men," but many of them are bad enough and they do distort both style and meaning. I have to assume, though, that you already know more than a few of these examples yourself.

But we would have to live on another planet not to know how successful the radical feminists have been in trying to impose this artificial kind of inclusive language on our society. Although the results of trying to use this unnatural kind of language are frequently clumsy and sometimes even absurd, many people today still go on— "manfully," we might say—trying to use it. People are even prone to apologize when, as inevitably happens they sometimes cannot help lapsing back into standard English.

Standard dictionaries now accept inclusive language, giving "male human being" as the first definition of "man." Teachers teach it; style books for the press and media require it; schools and universities demand it of their students writing term papers. Indeed, most of the leaders of society at large today—politicians, judges, TV anchors, newspaper editors, talking heads, academics, university presidents, army generals, navy admirals, CEOs, ministers of religion, and, sadly, not a few Catholic bishops as well—all hasten to pay their obeisance to the radical feminists by approving inclusive language.

In this climate, perhaps we should not be surprised that the International Commission on English in the Liturgy also decided— entirely on its own authority, by the way—"to avoid words which ignore the place of women in the Christian community altogether or which seem to relegate women to a secondary role." Nothing would do, in the minds of the ICEL translators but that the liturgy of the Catholic Church should henceforth be celebrated using inclusive language. What this meant was that, in addition to being freely translated in accordance with the principles of "dynamic equivalence," liturgical translations into English would henceforth also be crafted in accordance with radical feminist standards as well.

According to a volume prepared by ICEL itself, *Shaping English Liturgy* (Washington, DC: the Pastoral Press, 1990), the organization began using inclusive language in its translations of Roman liturgical texts from Latin into English as early as 1975. Initially, ICEL received full Church approval—including Roman approval—for such texts as the 1985 Order of Funerals, which it translated using inclusive language. The same thing was true of the initial segments of a revision of the Roman Missal which ICEL began translating as part of the "second generation" of translations to be used in the liturgy in English. The first ICEL offerings for the revision of the revised Roman Missal were fairly routinely—indeed, almost automatically—approved by large majorities of the American bishops, and were then sent on to Rome for final approval. This was pretty much the established pattern through most of the post-conciliar years: just as the bishops tended to be generally accepting of what their "professionals" and "experts" came up with, so this proved for a long time to be true of what the ICEL translators came up with.

This raises the general question of why the bishops, as the official guardians of the liturgy—as Vatican Council II had specifically confirmed—were so relatively passive and permissive in going along with whatever the ICEL translators happened to come up with—if, indeed, some bishops were not themselves proponents of the new translation standards! Yet from the very beginning of the institution of the vernacular liturgy, the typical ICEL translations were not only inferior; they were inaccurate and sometimes included actual omissions of what was plainly contained in the Latin text; indeed, they were sometimes outright mistranslations. Then, added to this, came the adoption of inclusive language by ICEL.

The bishops were never consulted about any of this; but then, with rare exceptions, they never seemed to have objected to it, either. Why were what seem in retrospect to have been so many mis-steps, mistakes, and outright errors so readily and easily tolerated?

There is no easy answer to these questions. Both at the Council and in the immediate post-conciliar period, too much was happening too fast in too many areas of the Church's life for the average bishop even to keep up with, much less control. In one important sense, the bishops had to depend upon what the experts and professionals were doing, since they could scarcely do it all themselves. Nobody at the time really knew how to effect a complete reform of the Church's liturgy, including the translation of all the liturgical texts from Latin into the vernacular. Much necessarily had to be improvised as various questions and problems arose. If in retrospect there is any blame to be assigned, perhaps the most significant failing of the Church's hierarchy lay in their choice of experts and professionals to rely on—and the continued toleration and employment of some of them after their true colors had become apparent.

The Instructions that began issuing from the Roman Congregations even before the Council was over, and later, as far as the liturgy was concerned, from Pope Paul VI's special Consilium, certainly read then, and mostly still read today, as if everything was being done in proper order; and as if careful thought was being given to at least the most important questions as they arose. Yet, looking back, we can see how deficient a liturgical reform was that allowed an area as large and as important as proper liturgical translations to be governed by a document as questionable and defective as *Comme le Prévoit*. The bishops of the English-speaking world seem to have accepted without serious examination or questions the translations provided by ICEL. More than that, when questions did arise which they had to take a closer look at, the tendency was still to approve and endorse pretty much what the experts had decided upon.

IV.

What happened to break ICEL's hold on liturgical translations? What happened, in December, 1992, to change the Church's course decisively with regard to translations into English, grew out of the issuance by Pope John Paul II of the *Catechism of the Catholic Church*. At the time the *Catechism* was promulgated, efforts were already in progress to have the work translated into both Latin and the major modern languages. Originally the *Catechism* had been written in French, which was the common language of the document's bishop-drafters. It was fully expected that English-speaking Catholics, among others, would soon have their own version of the *Catechism*. Inexplicably, however, the appearance of the English-language version of the *Catechism* kept being delayed. The *Catechism* did not appear in English, in fact, until May 27, 1994, nearly a year and a half after the original French version promulgated by the pope.

It turned out that the original English translation of the document had been done by a translator who had used *inclusive language*! When the Roman Congregations, particularly the Congregation for the Doctrine of the Faith, saw the distortions in meaning that resulted from this failed attempt to translate the *Catechism* using inclusive language, the Holy See demurred and insisted that a wholly new English translation of the *Catechism* had to be prepared. An Australian archbishop, the late Joseph Eric D'Arcy of Hobart, Tasmania, was commissioned to prepare a wholly new translation using standard English. (For an extended account of the whole question of the translation of the *Catechism* into English, see the chapter, "The Translation of the *Catechism* into English," in Wrenn, Michael J., and Whitehead, Kenneth D., *Flawed Expectations: The Reception of the Catechism of the Catholic Church*, San Francisco: Ignatius Press, 1996. The text of this book available on www.christendom-awake.org)

Confronted with an extensive text in English using inclusive language, the Holy See could not avoid seeing and judging its glaring inadequacies as a document of faith. Inclusive language does not really work. Once this was realized in Rome, the stage was set for a thorough re-examination of the existing scriptural and liturgical translations into English that had employed inclusive language, in particular those prepared by ICEL—but not only those prepared by ICEL since most biblical scholars too had long since taken up the ideological feminist cause and were producing scriptural translations using inclusive language.

The re-examination of the whole language question by Rome was not long in coming. In the fall of 1994, the Congregation for the Doctrine of the Faith requested that the approval of the New Revised Standard Version (NRSV) and the Revised New American Bible (RNAB) in English, which had been routinely granted two years earlier, be rescinded. This rescission directly affected, among other things, the revised new Lectionary with Scripture readings for the Mass based on the RNAB which was being translated. Up to this point the American bishops (although in slowly diminishing numbers) had been routinely and perhaps even automatically approving translations whether done by biblical scholars or ICEL.

Soon afterwards, the Congregation for Divine Worship and the Discipline of the Sacraments began holding up the ICEL liturgical translations submitted by the American bishops for the Roman *recognitio*, or approval. The Congregation even began sending some of them back. Throughout the 1990s, in fact, there was a complex and even confused series of liturgical texts going back and forth between Rome and the United States. It would be tedious, if it were even possible, to trace all of this movement in detail, but it is no exaggeration to say that, by the mid-1990s, it was becoming clear that Rome was no longer going to approve routinely the liturgical texts in English being submitted. ICEL was in trouble.

I believe Helen Hitchcock is going to tell you about the changes in the Congregation for Divine Worship and the Discipline of the Sacraments that took place in the 1990s and that helped bring about this new situation. This was particularly true following the appointment, in 1996, as pro-prefect, and two years later, as prefect, of the Congregation, of the former archbishop of Santiago, Jorge Arturo Medina Estevez. Although he only served for six years in this capacity, Cardinal Medina quite decisively changed things for the better on the liturgical translation front, among other things setting in motion a long overdue, badly needed, fundamental reform of ICEL. Cardinal Francis Arinze has ably continued the work of Cardinal Medina up to the present day.

As I say, Helen Hitchcock will have more to say on this particular topic, and I will only note here the irony that it was a Chilean cardinal—along with the German cardinal who was the prefect of the Congregation for the Doctrine of the Faith at the time!—who both perceived the need for and set the Church on the road to what we may now hope will before long be a new set of sound and sane translations of the Roman liturgy into English.

The American bishops, meanwhile, as it became more and more clear that Rome was no longer going to approve pretty much routinely the ICEL liturgical texts being submitted, became progressively more anxious and expended enormous efforts in Rome trying to get approved ICEL-translated texts that were more than dubious. In one dramatic instance, on December 13, 1996, all seven of the American cardinals active at the time went to Rome together in a body to lobby for the approval of a proposed new Lectionary based on the RNAB—the Bible translation from which Rome had withdrawn its approval. That *this* was the cause that could bring all seven of the active American cardinals to Rome together unfortunately speaks volumes about their priorities.

Early the next year, 1997, another delegation of American bishops went to Rome and sat down with Curia officials to work out a compromise on modified inclusive language for the new Lectionary. The compromise they achieved may have solved the immediate problem of an impasse between the American bishops and Rome, but their product proved to be far from entirely satisfactory.

At the same time, an increasing number of American bishops were themselves now actually beginning to question the adequacy of the translations which, formerly, had been almost automatically approved—first, by the Bishops' Committee on the Liturgy (BCL), and then by large majorities of bishops in the conference. But a new wind was now blowing, and it was increasingly coming to be understood that not only could ICEL-type translations no longer be given virtual rubber-stamp approval, some of them could not longer be approved at all; and more and more American bishops were coming to see the reasons for this. The stage was being set for developments that would eventually show that at long last that the Church finally *was* beginning to learn how to do liturgical translations properly.

We now need to chronicle, if only very briefly, the development of a new set of translation Norms by Rome both to supersede *Comme le Prévoit* and eliminate inclusive language; and, finally, we also need to take grateful note of the issuance of the Fifth Instruction on the Right Implementation of the Constitution on the Sacred liturgy, *Liturgiam Authenticam*, which will henceforth govern liturgical translations.

V.

The Roman Norms for the Translation of Biblical Texts for use in the Liturgy were developed and completed around 1995, and were probably already in use when the contingent of U.S. cardinals went to Rome to make their last-ditch plea for inclusive language. It was already too late. Rome was on the case. The new Norms were not at first made public, but were merely communicated to the bishops and ICEL translators. However, they were leaked to the *National Catholic Reporter* and caused a furor in liturgical circles when they were published.

Among other things, the new Norms constitute practically a point-by-point annulling of a set of Criteria for the Evaluation of Inclusive Language Translations of Scriptural Texts Proposed for Liturgical Use that the U.S. bishops had issued in 1990. The bishops and their scholars and experts, concerned that "justice" be done to women, had sanctioned so-called "horizontal" inclusive language (that is, when God was not directly being referred to); "vertical" references to God or Jesus would supposedly continue with standard English, according to these bishops' Criteria. While the new Vatican translation Norms did not even mention inclusive language by name, they effectively swept all this away.

Specifically, the new Vatican Translation Norms require: 1) accurate translations made with (2) "maximum possible fidelity to the words of the text" and "faithful to the sense of sacred Scripture understood as a unity and totality." Translations must (3) "faithfully reflect the Word of God in the original languages…without 'correction' or 'improvement' in the service of modern sensitivities.'" In cases of obscurity, translations should be made (3a) with "due regard" to the Church's Latin Neo-Vulgate Bible; and, if explanations are necessary, they should be given (3b) in appended notes, not incorporated into the translated text.

Vatican Translation Norm 4 is subdivided into six subparts, each of which prohibits a specific translation malpractice: (4 § 1) "the natural gender of *personae* in the Bible…must not be changed"; (4 § 2) "the grammatical gender of God, pagan deities, angels, and demons…must not be changed"; (4 § 3) "in fidelity to the inspired Word of God, the traditional biblical usage for naming the persons of the Trinity as Father, Son, and Holy Spirit is to be retained"; (4 § 4) "…in keeping with the Church's tradition, the feminine and the neuter pronouns are not to be used to refer to the person of the Holy Spirit"; (4 § 5) "there shall be no systematic substitution of the masculine pronoun or possessive adjective to refer to God in correspondence to the original text"; and (4 § 6); "kinship terms that are clearly gender specific…should be respected in translation."

Each of these subparts of Vatican Translation Norm 4 prohibits a specific and favored ICEL translation practice identified from various inclusive-language translations submitted to the Holy See. Observance of this six-part Norm alone would by itself eliminate most of the errors in such translations as the NRSV and the RNAB. Taken together, these prohibitions would eliminate such errors as substituting "Creator, Redeemer, and Sanctifier" for "Father, Son, and Holy Spirit"; avoiding the use of masculine pronouns referring to God by repeating the word God; referring to the Holy Spirit as "she" or "it."; or changing the natural or the grammatical genders found in original texts.

Vatican Translation Norm 5 follows up on this last point and specifies that "grammatical number and person in the original texts should ordinarily be maintained." What this means is that the practice of switching to the plural, "they," in order to avoid having to use the generic "he," is eliminated. This is one of the most common practices in inclusive language translations, of course, and it often results in serious mistranslations; for it cannot be maintained that the plural always means the same thing as the singular. With regard to the religious meaning, the Christological dimension may be lost in many Old Testament texts which prefigure Christ or refer to his coming (as Norm 6 § 2 below also points out) when singulars are changed to plurals.

Translation Norm 6 is divided into three subparts, the first of which (6 § 1) specifies that "translations should strive to preserve the connotations as well as the denotations of words or expressions in the original, and not preclude possible layers of meaning." This subpart is evidently intended to eliminate errors such as those which inevitably arise when translators focus upon preoccupations such as "male dominance, and thereby ignore other important nuances and layers of meaning. Norm (6 § 2) notes that "...where the New Testament of the Church's tradition has interpreted certain texts in the Old Testament in a Christological fashion, special care should be observed in the translation of these texts so that Christological meaning is not precluded." Finally, Norm (6 § 3) says that the word "man" in English should translate [Hebrew] *'adam* and [Greek] *anthropos*, since there is no one synonym which effectively conveys the play between the individual, the collectivity, and the unity of the human family..."

All in all, then, these new Vatican translation Norms reflect a sane and realistic view of what is required in liturgical translations, even in the present heightened and ideological atmosphere. We must be grateful for the clear-sightedness of the Roman congregations; they were finally able to see how the acceptance of the inclusive language, along with the other features of "dynamic equivalence" in translations, was deforming and debasing the Church's liturgy—and this at a time when most English-speaking bishops, along with their *periti* and probably the majority of today's biblical scholars, were generally not seeing this at all but were just going along with the supposed demands of today's secular culture and the radical feminist movement..

All of this was brought to fruition when the Holy See's Fifth Instruction on the Right Implementation of the Constitution on the Sacred Liturgy, *Liturgiam Authenticam* ("Authentic Liturgy"), was published with the date of March 28, 2001 (having been approved by Pope John Paul II on March 20, 2001). *Liturgiam Authenticam* truly does inaugurate a new era in the use of the vernacular liturgy. This Instruction brings together and lays out systematically in one authoritative document all the points and corrections which Rome was engaged in making piece-meal in the course of the 1990s.

The document expressly aims to correct what it calls omissions and errors which affect certain vernacular translations" (LA 6); and it declares its intention of establishing "anew the true notion of liturgical translation in order that the translations of the sacred liturgy into the vernacular languages may stand secure as the authentic voice of the Church of God" (LA 7).

In this Roman document, we find both solid general principles applicable to all translations, and specific norms which go into enough salutary detail to exclude the kinds of defects found in past ICEL liturgical texts. In particular, the new Vatican Translation Norms summarized above are fully incorporated into the document, almost word for word. *Liturgiam Authenticam* even goes farther and specifies that "the term 'fathers' found in many biblical passages and liturgical texts of ecclesiastical composition, is to be rendered by the corresponding masculine word into vernacular languages insofar as it may be seen to refer to the patriarchs or the kings of the chosen people in the Old Testament" (LA 31). This will entail another change, since for some time now we have been hearing about our "ancestors" instead of our "fathers."

In summary, all this has been a long time in coming, around forty years, but with this new Roman document, we can truly say that the Church finally has now learned how to do liturgical translations.

The indications are that the new "generation" of liturgical texts in English now being crafted by a reformed ICEL in accordance with the Church's new translation standards will in fact be a huge improvement over what we have had up to now. *Speremus.*

> Liturgical translation, according to *Liturgiam Authenticam*:
> …is not so much a work of creative innovation as it is of rendering the original texts faithfully and accurately into the vernacular language. While it is permissible to arrange the wording, syntax, and the style in such a way as to prepare a flowing vernacular text suitable to the rhythm of popular prayer, the original text, insofar as possible, must be translated integrally and in the most exact manner, without omissions or additions in terms of their content, and without paraphrases or glosses (LA 29).

We can surely all say "Amen" to that!

Kenneth D. Whitehead is the author of hundreds of articles in Catholic publications as well as of a number of books, notably, *One, Holy, Catholic, and Apostolic: The Early Church Was the Catholic Church* (Ignatius Press, 2000). A new, revised and updated edition of the book he co-authored in 1981, *The Pope, the Council, and the Mass*, was published by Emmaus Road Publishing in 2006. He is the editor of a number of other volumes, including, most recently, *The Church, Marriage, and the Family* (St. Augustine's Press, 2007). He has translated more than 20 books from French, German, or Italian, including Archbishop Agostino Marchetto's major work *Il Concilio Ecumenico Vaticano II.*

Mr. Whitehead was educated at the University of Utah and the University of Paris, and holds an honorary decree as Doctor of Christian Letters from the Franciscan University of Steubenville. He is a recipient of the Cardinal Wright Award from the Fellowship of Catholic Scholars, the Blessed Frederic Ozanam Award from the Society of Catholic Social Scientists, the Humanitarian Award from the American Maritain Association, and (with his wife Margaret) the Faith and Family Award from Women for Faith and Family. He is currently a member of the board of directors of the Fellowship of Catholic Scholars and for several years has served as editor of the annual FCS "Proceedings," including the present volume.

X.

Session IV
Redemptionis Sacramentum –
A New Era of Liturgical Reform

Beginning the "New Era of Liturgical Renewal"

Helen Hull Hitchcock

> *Every liturgical celebration, because it is an action of Christ the Priest and of His Body which is the Church, is a sacred action surpassing all others; no other action of the Church can equal its efficacy by the same title and to the same degree.*
>
> *In the earthly Liturgy we take part in a foretaste of that Heavenly Liturgy which is celebrated in the holy city of Jerusalem toward which we journey as pilgrims, where Christ is sitting at the right hand of God, a Minister of the Holies and of the true Tabernacle; we sing a hymn to the Lord's glory with all the warriors of the heavenly army; venerating the memory of the saints, we hope for some part and fellowship with them; we eagerly await the Savior, Our Lord Jesus Christ, until He, our Life, shall appear and we too will appear with Him in glory.*
>
> —*Sacrosanctum Concilium 7, 8*

With this stirring statement, the Fathers of the Second Vatican Council announced the fundamental goal of the reform of the "earthly Liturgy," to make it more transparent to the "cosmic Liturgy"—to "a foretaste of that Heavenly Liturgy toward which we journey" This goal has been pursued but not achieved in the more than four decades since these words were published. Milestones like anniversaries prompt us to review our experience of the past, and, with the benefit of this experience, good or ill, to proceed—even if the way before us may still not seem entirely clear. Yet experience is what we have, and if we are willing to learn from this history, we may discover it to be diagnostic, corrective, and beneficial. We need to get our bearings so that we can set our pilgrim course.

Review: The Mass in English – 1963-1989

On November 22, 1963, the day President John Kennedy was assassinated, the fathers of the Second Vatican Council approved its first document, the Constitution on the Sacred Liturgy, *Sacrosanctum Concilium*. It was released officially on December 3, 1963.

The International Commission on English in the Liturgy (ICEL), the "mixed commission" that would provide vernacular liturgical texts for all English-speaking countries, had already been organized in October, principally by Archbishop Paul Hallinan of Atlanta.

Pope Paul VI appointed the Consilium, a committee of experts whose task was to oversee the implementation of *Sacrosanctum Concilium*—and to initiate the most sweeping changes in the liturgy in the Church's history. This they went about accomplishing in great haste.

Within a year, a new version of the Missal, with parts in the vernacular as permitted in *Sacrosanctum Concilium,* was published. And ICEL had already begun working on a revision that would be entirely in English.

In November, 1968—distracted by the disruptions of anti-war demonstrators and preoccupied with the disturbing rebellion within the Church that had erupted when Pope Paul VI's encyclical, *Humanae Vitae,* appeared that June—the U.S. bishops quickly approved ICEL's translation of the new Order of Mass. The bishops' vote was taken on November 11; the Holy See granted its approval on November 13; and on November 15, the conference mandated that the new texts must be in use by January 1, 1969. Pope Paul VI promulgated the complete new Missal a few months later.

Other translation projects proceeded at similar breakneck speed. Several new English translations of the Bible were published almost as soon as the Constitution on Divine Revelation, *Dei Verbum,* appeared. This was another historic change for Catholics. Since 1572, when the first English translation of the Latin Vulgate provided English-speaking Catholics with the Scriptures in their own language, there had been only relatively minor changes in the Douay Bible. A new translation of the Vulgate by Ronald Knox was published in the late 1940s, but it was short-lived. The Jerusalem Bible, an English edition of an earlier French version, was published in 1966; the Revised Standard Version–Catholic Edition was also published in 1966; and the New American Bible was in print by 1970. These three new translations of the Bible were employed in the new, expanded Lectionaries.

One example of the euphoric "open windows" mood of the time that affects the liturgy today was ICEL's rush to produce "ecumenical texts." In 1969, ICEL convened an ecumenical group of translators as the International Consultation on Common Texts (ICET). Its objective was to produce common liturgical texts in English for the Eucharist and other worship services for a variety of member churches. Several ICET texts are currently in use in the Catholic Church (*inter alia*, the Nicene Creed, *Kyrie, Gloria, Te Deum*).[1]

In the same year the Consilium produced a document to provide principles for translation of liturgical texts; it was known as *Comme le Prévoit* ("As foreseen…"). It would be used to justify "dynamically equivalent" renderings of English texts for more than thirty years—until it was replaced by *Liturgiam Authenticam* in 2001.

Almost before the ink was dry on the first set of translations, new versions and revisions were produced, following the principles of *Comme le Prévoit.* The ICEL translation of the new *Missale Romanum,* called the "Sacramentary," appeared in 1973-74, and it is still in use today with a few changes. But new projects and revisions were already in progress.

The usual procedure for approval of these new texts was brief. The Liturgical Commission of the U.S. bishops' conference, later the Bishops' Committee on the Liturgy (BCL), had a very free rein to propose new texts to the bishops—and not all of these texts were actually presented to the entire bishops' conference for debate and a vote, but rather were approved by the conference's Administrative Board, or simply by the Liturgy Committee alone. Even when the full body of bishops did vote, their approval was essentially pro forma. The Consilium group in Rome routinely approved the publication of the new liturgical texts on behalf of the Holy See.

Liturgical Bureaucracy Mushrooms

Meanwhile, a formidable bureaucracy was being created in the United States. Diocesan liturgy commissions were quickly appearing, and the bishops' Liturgical Commission organized these into the Federation of Diocesan Liturgical Commissions (FDLC). This group was encouraged to make "resolutions" and "proposals for action" that would be given to the Liturgical Commission (later BCL) for action.

The decade following the Council also saw massive production of other new liturgical translations and the multiplication of new projects that were launched and rushed into use. The publishing of these texts (and often "contemporary music" to accompany them) became an independent industry. The "liturgical industrial complex" was born.

The confusion that prevailed in these years is hard to overstate. Bishops were overwhelmed by the complexity of procedures, blurred lines of authority, burgeoning bureaucracy at the national and diocesan levels, the multiplicity of new academic programs for the study of the liturgy, and new publishing ventures to produce the new liturgical books. All of this was further compounded by the growing and distracting political cacophony, and the prevailing atmosphere of rebellion in the secular world and in the Church that characterized the 1960s and 1970s. It is not hard to see why most bishops came to rely very heavily on liturgical experts. Bishops were often not fully aware of what was going on with the liturgy even in their own chanceries, to say nothing of the national conference. Archbishop (later Cartdinal) John Krol of Philadelphia, who was president of the national Conference at the time, famously remarked, "I can either run the Conference or the Church in Philadelphia. Not both."

Confronted by a continuous cascade of new texts, new directives, free-wheeling liturgical experimentation (apparently authorized by the Consilium), and the consolidation of power in the "interlocking directorates" of ICEL, the BCL, the Consilium and its chosen experts, it would have been impossible for even the most conscientious bishop to exercise any effective control of the process. Most did not even try.

By the late 1970s, the liturgical establishment that had freely formed itself with no effective opposition was very deeply entrenched, and almost completely independent of any ecclesiastical control; often it was enriched by royalties from the many books that were now required for Catholic worship. In truth, this liturgical establishment was answerable to no one. It had learned to expect no interference from any quarter—from the pope on down. Like the parallel developments within catechetics and Catholic academic institutions, the liturgical establishment was in thrall to its own notion of "freedom" and "reform" and "the Spirit of Vatican II."

Since every innovation was presented as the will of the bishops and of Rome, sweeping changes in Catholic liturgical practice were accomplished, in many cases, quite literally overnight. It evidently rarely occurred to anyone to question the motives of the individuals who engineered these changes. People had been convinced that obedience to the highest Church authority required their acceptance of any and all liturgical innovations introduced. Furthermore, as Cardinal Joseph Ratzinger later observed, since most people privately recited prayers during most of the Mass, this probably contributed to their indifference when the old liturgical books disappeared: "People had never been in contact with the liturgy itself," he said, though exceptions to this indifference were found in places where the "Liturgical Movement had created a certain love for the Liturgy [and] anticipated the essential ideas of the Council, as for example the praying participation of all in the liturgical action."[2]

Ideology Invades Translations

But an even greater problem had developed than the dizzying profusion of changes in the Liturgy, although few were conscious of it. It reflected—and paralleled—the secular "cultural revolution" that had pervaded nearly all sectors of the Church, and was especially notable in religious orders.

By 1975, ICEL's translators, and others as well, had adopted ideology-driven theories of translation, to which all its subsequent alterations in the language of the English liturgy would conform. Feminists (some of them ICEL members) claimed that the English language itself was "patriarchal," and anti-woman, and they demanded that liturgical and biblical texts must be revised as a matter of "justice" to women.[3]

Sometimes the texts of the Mass were changed, by-passing the vote of the body of bishops. One notable instance of this was omitting the word "men" from the institution narrative in all Eucharistic Prayers. The translation of *pro multis* (literally "for many) was rendered "for all men" in the original 1973 version. The change to "for all" was approved and incorporated into the official text of all the Eucharistic Prayers in 1981[4]—a seemingly a small change, "a cloud no bigger than a man's hand," but it signaled a commitment to the feminist agenda, as well as demonstrating the influence of feminists within the Church, which would pervade all further translation projects throughout the decade of the 1990s.

ICEL's policy is clear from a 1983 statement on the rejection of a new Grail translation of the Psalter that had systematically eliminated all "exclusive language." The statement was made by Cincinnati Archbishop Daniel Pilarcyk, then president of the ICEL Episcopal Board. He wrote that his ICEL Committee had emphatically affirmed the Liturgy Committee's commitment to the revised Grail Psalter and to the new liturgical language:

> The [bishops' conference] has favored the use of inclusive language in liturgical texts and has approved such language since 1978…Non-authorization of the revised Grail Psalter at this time should not be construed as insensitivity to the question …The [Committee] maintains its commitment to those plans and projects of [ICEL] in which liturgical texts are revised or translated with inclusive language in mind.
> The [Committee] applauds and commends the work of The Grail in this … carefully revised inclusive-language version of the Psalter…[and] looks forward to [its] publication…
> Finally, the [Committee] wishes to make it known that the question of inclusive language is a matter that deserves attention in the Church because of the cultural

development of the English language …The [Committee] intends to commission a scholarly review of the elements inherent in the inclusive language issue. The [Committee] does not understand the matter of inclusive language as a "women's issue" only…Rather, the [Committee] understands inclusive language to be a question of the cultural development of the English language and therefore important to all worshiping members of the Church. It is the hope of the [Committee]…that an inclusive language version of the Psalter be authorized for liturgical use in the dioceses of the United States…[5]

Although in 1993 the vote of the bishops' conference would *reject* the gender-neutered Grail Psalter for *liturgical use,* the Liturgy Committee's report from the November, 1991, conference says the BCL "agreed to re-examine the revised Grail Psalter (Inclusive Language Version) and will establish a mechanism to recommend to the publisher changes required by the "Criteria for the Evaluation of Inclusive Language Translations," and that "once all the problems have been satisfactorily resolved, the Committee will recommend that the NCCB authorize this version of the Psalter for liturgical use."[6]

The Pope Reviews the Reform.

The problems with the reform of the liturgy according to the Council's mandate were not confined to America or the English-speaking world. Pope John Paul II recognized this. In a 1981 letter for a meeting of the Italian Center for Liturgical Action, Cardinal Augustino Casaroli, the Vatican Secretary of State, had expressed Pope John Paul II's view that while the liturgical reform "has intended to put forth valid premises for the reflourishing of the spiritual life of the Christian community…It cannot be hidden, however, that the genuine conciliar orientation has often been disregarded, with doctrinal attitudes and practices in contrast to the principles and directives of the same liturgical reform". He continued as follows:

In some cases, there has been underestimated the danger of a progressive and fatal slipping away from the sacredness of the liturgy, by including in it forms which alter its significance and its substance; often there has been neglected the link with tradition, with the consequent risk of betraying the very contents of the liturgical action; at times, by abusing the creative possibilities offered by the new rituals, there have been imposed on the faithful experiments which have nothing to do with the demands of noble simplicity and the essence of the Church's liturgy.

The letter expresses hope that these "deplorable abuses" will be overcome, and encourages "authentic workers" and initiatives that "have striven with genuine authenticity to bring the liturgy near to the people of God and to elevate the faithful to the liturgical mystery and liturgical language".[7]

On the 25th anniversary of the Council's Constitution on the Sacred Liturgy in 1988, Pope John Paul II drew attention to continuing and deepening problems with the first phase of the post-Conciliar liturgical reform. In his apostolic letter, *Vicesimus Quintus Annos*, released in May, 1989, the pope reaffirmed the principles for reform contained in *Sacrosanctum Concilium;* but he also pointed out that "the application of the liturgical reform has met with difficulties due especially to an unfavorable environment marked by a tendency to see religious practice as something of a private affair," and he deplored "outlandish innovations, departing from the norms issued by the Apostolic See or the bishops, thus disrupting the unity of the Church and the piety of the faithful, and even...contradicting matters of faith. (VQA 11). He wrote further:

> On occasion, there have been noted illicit omissions or additions, rites invented outside the framework of established norms; postures or songs which are not conducive to faith or to a sense of the sacred; abuses in the practice of general absolution; confusion between the ministerial priesthood, linked with ordination, and the common priesthood of the faithful, which has its foundation in baptism.
>
> It cannot be tolerated that certain priests should take upon themselves the right to compose Eucharistic Prayers or to substitute profane readings for texts from Sacred Scripture. Initiatives of this sort, far from being linked with the liturgical reform as such, or with the books which have issued from it, are in direct contradiction to it, disfigure it

and deprive the Christian people of the genuine treasures of the Liturgy of the Church.

It is for the bishops to root out such abuses, because the regulation of the Liturgy depends on the bishop within the limits of the law, and because "the life in Christ of His faithful people in some sense is derived from and depends upon him" (VQA 13).

The pope also stressed the responsibility of the episcopal conferences for providing accurate translations of liturgical books:

The episcopal conferences have had the weighty responsibility of preparing the translations of the liturgical books. Immediate need occasionally led to the use of provisional translations, approved ad interim. But now the time has come to reflect upon certain difficulties that have subsequently emerged, to remedy certain defects or inaccuracies, to complete partial translations, to compose or approve chants to be used in the liturgy, to ensure respect for the texts approved and lastly to publish liturgical books in a form that both testifies to the stability achieved and is worthy of the mysteries being celebrated.

For the work of translation, as well as for the wider implications of liturgical renewal for whole countries, each episcopal conference was required to establish a national commission and ensure the collaboration of experts in the various sectors of liturgical science and pastoral practice. The time has come to evaluate this commission, its past activity, both the positive and negative aspects, and the guidelines and the help which it has received from the episcopal conference regarding its composition and activity. The role of this commission is much more delicate when the conference wishes to introduce certain measures of adaptation or inculturation: this is one more reason for making sure that the commission contains people who are truly competent (VQA 20).

But these admonitions—especially evaluating translation commissions and their objective — would have little immediate effect. Seven months after the Pope's letter appeared, Bishop Joseph Delaney, chairman of the BCL, addressed the 20th anniversary meeting of the Federation of Diocesan Liturgical Commissions (FDLC), on October 11, 1989, on the forthcoming revision of the Roman Missal (ICEL Sacramentary), and a second edition of the Lectionary for Mass. Bishop Delaney's address, published in the *FDLC Newsletter,* said that "ICEL hopes to have its work [on the two-volume Sacramentary] done by 1992"; and, concerning the BCL Lectionary Subcommittee, "changes are being made to *insure the use of inclusive language.* To this end the subcommittee is following the principles that have been enunciated by the Joint Committee [BCL and Doctrine Committees] in "Inclusive Language in Biblical Translations." Every effort has been made to address *each particular instance of exclusive language* and insofar as it is possible, inclusive language has been substituted" (emphasis added). Bishop Delaney also announced that work on a Lectionary for Masses with Children was nearing completion.

In November, 1990, the U.S. bishops issued "Criteria for the Evaluation of Inclusive Language Translations of Scriptural Texts proposed for Liturgical Use." These Criteria were produced by the Joint Committee (Liturgy and Doctrine)—fifteen years after ICEL began to employ feminist language as a guiding principle for all liturgical translations, and just at the beginning of a highly intense period of proposed new translations of both biblical and liturgical texts.

The following year, a new Lectionary was accepted by the Bishops, incorporating the "gender inclusive language" of the revised New American Bible (NAB), the Scripture translation used for the Lectionary in the United States.[8] At the November, 1991, bishops' meeting, in a special statement to the bishops on the NAB Psalter revision policy by the unnamed "Revisers and Steering Committee," the Criteria guidelines are referenced. The anonymous writers say that changing the text is "urgent" and is "legitimate, for it gives the sense and does not violate our sensibilities":

> When Hebrew uses the third person masculine in generalized contexts, it is used as it formerly was used in English, i.e., in an inclusive sense. But since in English it *no longer has that inclusive sense,* to render it as third person masculine would not be a literal translation (i.e., one which gives the true meaning of the text) but a mistranslation.
> In the case of horizontal language, our revision of the

Psalter avoids exclusive language by various means; most often this is by resorting to the plural…

The case of vertical language is more difficult. The Bible depicts God in predominantly masculine terms, and no attempt is made to change the imagery of king, warrior, shepherd, etc. The use of the masculine pronoun is somewhat different. The revision committee proceeded on the conviction that the bishops would agree that *urgent pastoral needs override the demand for strict literalism.* To that end we *eliminate the use of the masculine pronoun for God* where it can be done gracefully…

Taking into account the primary concern of presenting a Psalter for use in the liturgy, noting the Bishops' *grave pastoral concern,* and intending to make this revision respond to the needs of our day, we believe the means we have used to make the language of this revision inclusive are legitimate.[9]

Obviously the members of ICEL and the U.S. bishops' Committee on Liturgy were of one mind regarding the principal objectives of renovation of liturgical texts.

But feminist-inspired tampering with the Bible was not the only problem. Also at their Fall, 1991, meeting, the U.S. bishops officially approved a Lectionary for Masses with Children using the text of an American Bible Society translation, called the "Contemporary English Version" (that became known in the pressroom as the "Away-in-a-Feedbox Bible"). This Lectionary's introduction states:

Upon publication, the Lectionary for Masses with Children will be the only approved lectionary for use at Masses with children in the dioceses of the United States of America.[10]

Although the bishops approved this "Children's Lectionary" as an interim text on condition that it be reviewed after five years, it remained in use for over fourteen years. A new version, now based on a "simplified" version of the NAB, was approved at the November 2005 bishops' meeting—with a caveat that it be used *only* at Masses when children in *primary school* (first through third grades) form the majority of the congregation.

At the same 1991 bishops' meeting, the Bishops' Liturgy Committee proposed granting permission for the creation of a new Lectionary based on the National Council of Churches' (NCC) New Revised Standard Version (NRSV), saying that "since the recently revised versions of these biblical translations use inclusive language, the Secretariat has received several requests that they now be authorized for liturgical use."[11] The Conference's Administrative Committee had already granted its *imprimatur* to the NRSV translation in September, 1991; so the bishops were in the awkward position of being asked to vote on a translation already given this form of approval. The NRSV handily secured the required two-thirds majority of the voting members of the conference. However, later, in 1994, the NRSV was expressly rejected by the Holy See for use in the liturgy.

Also during their November, 1991, meeting, the bishops established the Ad Hoc Committee for the Review of Scripture Translations, with authorization for this committee to approve biblical texts on behalf of the conference. This Committee's "approval" did not include liturgical use of these texts, however.

The following year, a new NAB-based Lectionary, created principally for the purpose of rendering its "outdated" English acceptable to feminists was introduced and overwhelmingly approved. This was at the June, 1992, meeting. The Revised NAB translations had already received the conference's *imprimatur* and *nihil obstat* through its Administrative Committee and the newly created Ad Hoc Committee. By the time these "theologically corrected" translations reached the floor of the bishops meeting, they were already, in effect, a *fait accompli,* although the plenary body of the bishops is expected to approve the work of its committees.

ICEL's Parallel Track

The history of the ICEL liturgical renewal project, as documented by its own members, reveals the following:

1) That commitment to so-called "inclusive" language had been its guiding principle since 1975;

2) That ICEL's decisions regarding all English translations of Scripture and prayers used in public worship had with very rare and minor exceptions

been accepted, virtually without question, by the
bishops' conferences;
3) That ICEL's committees were heavily influenced by
radical feminist theology and Scripture scholarship;
4) That only the eleven bishops on ICEL's Episcopal
Board routinely approved the work of an even
smaller number of people who actually produced these
translations; and,
5) That ICEL's commitment to "change," to a revisionist
theological and ecclesial position, was imposed
for years on millions of English-speaking Catholic
worshippers by the gradual incorporation of feminist-
language texts throughout the Church in English-
speaking countries.

Archbishop Daniel Pilarczyk, in his report on ICEL to the
NCCB at the November, 1991, meeting had confidently predicted that
ICEL's finances would be secure when the revision of the Sacramentary,
then in progress, was ready for distribution in about 1997.[12]

Inclusive language issues would continue to plague the many
translation projects throughout the 1990s—including the English
translation of *Catechism of the Catholic Church*, promulgated by the
Apostolic Constitution of the Holy Father on October 11, 1992, on
the 30th anniversary of the opening of the Second Vatican Council.
But a conflict over the English translation of the *Catechism* very soon
developed because of "inclusive language."

On the 30th anniversary of *Sacrosanctum Concilium,* December
4, 1993, in his ad limina address to a group of American bishops, Pope
John Paul II again stressed the importance of accurate translations. Not
only had the *Catechism* translation been delayed, but the enormous
project of retranslation and revision of all English-language liturgical
books, including both the Sacramentary and the Lectionary, was in
progress, and would occupy the U.S. bishops for the entire decade. In
his address to the US bishops, the Holy Father observed:

The arduous task of translation must guard the *full
doctrinal integrity* and, according to the genius of each
language, the beauty of the original texts. When so many
people are thirsting for the living God (Ps 42:2)—whose

majesty and mercy are at the heart of liturgical prayer—
the Church must respond with a *language of praise and
worship which fosters respect and gratitude for God's
greatness, compassion and power.* When the faithful gather
to celebrate the work of our redemption, the language of
her prayer—free from doctrinal ambiguity and ideological
influence—should foster the dignity and beauty of the
celebration itself, while faithfully expressing the Church's
faith and unity" (emphasis in the original).[13]

A few months later, the Fourth Instruction on Implementation
of the Council's Liturgical Reform, *Varietates Legitimae,* was
published by the Congregation for Divine Worship and the Discipline
of the Sacraments. The date was March 29, 1994. And the English
translation of the *Catechism of the Catholic Church,* carefully
corrected under the close supervision of the Congregation for the
Doctrine of the Faith, finally appeared in June, 1994.

During these years, many faithful Catholics, often dismayed
by years of unchecked liturgical innovations, became aware of the
proposed liturgical changes, revisions, and retranslations of biblical
and liturgical texts, and began to comprehend more acutely their own
responsibilities—not only as participants in Catholic worship, but
also transmitting the faith in its full integrity to future generations of
Catholics. As a result, new associations and movements of clergy and
laity were formed in order express fidelity to the Magisterium and to
foster a more profound sense of the sacred in Catholic worship. Several
of these initiatives focused primarily on issues involving the liturgy.[14]

It is not possible to mention here all the translations and
revisions that occupied the English-speaking Churches and the Holy
See, or that contributed directly to the development of "the new era
of liturgical renewal." But it was to be a "sea change," and it was
signaled by two major events at the beginning of the new millennium,
namely: 1) the appearance of the third typical edition of the *Missale
Romanum* in 2000 (though it would not be officially promulgated
until 2002); and 2) the Fifth Instruction on the Implementation of
Sacrosanctum Concilium, Liturgiam Authenticam, which was released
in 2001 by the Congregation for Divine Worship and the Discipline of

the Sacraments. We can summarize several key contributing factors related to these developments.

• The proposed revisions in English-language liturgical texts entailed gaining approval for the new texts from the bishops conferences, and this, in turn, gave the bishops an opportunity for far greater scrutiny to the proposals for change than they had had immediately following the Council. As a result of their years-long discussions of ICEL's Missal revisions, the bishops gained a new sense of their profound responsibility for the Church's liturgy, and many of them showed that they now fully understood the importance of accurate translations.

In 1993, the US bishops declined to vote on the first segment of ICEL's proposed revision of the Sacramentary, thus delaying the approval process for several years. The delay reflected the bishops' growing concern over the many new scriptural and liturgical texts and the process of approving them, and permitted more time for their consideration of new proposals. They submitted hundreds of amendments to ICEL's work, in fact, though most of them were rejected. In the end, though, many bishops showed that they had lost confidence in the system. However, they generally relied on the Holy See to make necessary corrections when the ICEL text was sent for *recognitio* in early 1998.

• The appearance of the *Catechism of the Catholic Church*, and the need to translate it correctly, brought into focus issues involved in producing accurate translations generally. The Holy See had to intervene in the case of the English version of the Catechism, published in 1994.

• Many new and revised English translations of Scripture appeared during the 1990s, as a response to the feminist demand for gender-neutered texts. All these Scripture texts, however, required approval by the Congregation for the Doctrine of the Faith for use in Catholic worship. Problems encountered with several of these Scripture texts resulted in the CDF's developing a set of interim "Norms for the Translation of Biblical Texts for Use in the Liturgy." These Norms were eventually published in 1997. They served as a precursor to *Liturgiam Authenticam,* which incorporated their basic principles.

The Medina Years

In June, 1996, Archbishop (later Cardinal) Jorge Arturo Medina Estévez was appointed pro-prefect of the Congregation for Divine Worship and the Discipline of the Sacraments. This Chilean archbishop had helped write the *Catechism of the Catholic Church*, had been a peritus at the Second Vatican Council, and was a member of the International Theological Commission for the Interpretation of Canon Law. At the time of his appointment, then-Archbishop Medina Estévez was quoted in an interview as saying:

> There is reason to lament the fact that some translations are not faithful but quite fanciful [*fantasiosi*]. I believe that the texts of the Leonine, Gregorian, and Gelasian sacramentaries have a perennial richness and value. And it is possible to translate them with fidelity. At times translation is confused with interpretation, but they are two different things.

That same month, at a meeting with Archbishop Pilarczyk, president of the ICEL Episcopal Board, Archbishop Geraldo Majella Agnelo, secretary of the Congregation for Divine Worship observed the need for changes since the "first period of liturgical reform," expressly pinpointing translations and *Comme le Prévoit:*

> *Comme le Prévoit* contains valuable principles but must be recognized as a text dated 1969, from the first period of liturgical reform. Its current value is therefore conditioned by the experience of the last 27 years, along with the fact that there exist new canon law norms regarding the approval of such translations.
>
> Perhaps along this line there is a need to make further clarification to the bishops' conferences, in order to increase their involvement and their influence in something that is their right and duty: translating liturgical books and texts."[15]

In July, 1996, a delegation of U.S. bishops met with Vatican officials on the need for correcting the revised Lectionary to accord with the CDF translation norms (which at that point had not been made public). And on December 13, all seven US cardinals met in Rome with the prefects of the Congregation for the Doctrine of the Faith (Cardinal Ratzinger) and the Congregation for Divine Worship and Discipline of the Sacraments (Archbishop Medina Estévez), reportedly to urge Vatican approval of the revised Lectionary "as soon as possible."

The result of these highly unusual meetings was that a working committee of US bishops and Vatican scholars was appointed to repair the "inclusivized" Lectionary text, which they did the following March.

Just before their June, 1997, meeting, the U.S. bishops received copies of the CDF "Norms on Scripture Translation," which conclusively rejected using "inclusive language" devices for Scripture translation—a direct and succinct rejection of *Comme le Prévoit.* Also at this 1997 meeting, the bishops were presented with the amended version of the Lectionary, and they voted on the final version of the ICEL's proposed Sacramentary revision.

On June 30 of that same year, Chicago Archbishop (later Cardinal) Francis George was appointed as the U.S. representative to the episcopal board of ICEL, replacing Cincinnati Archbishop Daniel Pilarczyk, who had served for eleven years.

Archbishop Medina had sent a landmark letter to the U.S. bishops' conference in September, 1997, informing them that ICEL's *Ordination Rite* submitted for the Holy See's approval had been definitively rejected. His letter cited serious problems with the ICEL text, and it was accompanied by a list of no less than 114 specific deficiencies, stressing that this list of deficiencies was not "exhaustive."

His letter strongly signaled the Congregation's profound seriousness in exercising the Holy See's responsibility and authority to oversee the renewal of the Sacred Liturgy, to urge the bishops to accept their own responsibility, and to intervene, whenever necessary, to assure the authentic renewal of the Sacred Liturgy, as the Council intended.

In January, 1998, the ICEL Sacramentary was finally submitted to the CDW for *recognitio.* The following month, Archbishop Medina was elevated to the cardinalate, that is, on February 21.

During the next two years, the U.S. bishops conference was occupied with more revisions of the Lectionary, which became the focus of increasing controversy over the direction of the Liturgy now being provided by Rome.

Dawn of the "New Era"

In October, 1999, nearly a year after the ICEL Sacramentary had been submitted to the CDW, Cardinal Medina Estévez called for a thoroughgoing reform of ICEL's procedures and structure, and directed that ICEL reform its governing statutes.

In a letter to Bishop Maurice Taylor, president of the Episcopal Board of ICEL, the cardinal noted that English-language liturgical translation problems "assume a particular gravity" because the impact of English on other language groups is "an observed and unavoidable fact".[16] Cardinal Medina's letter said that ICEL's revised statutes should be submitted by Easter, 2000, and he confirmed the Holy See's mission of oversight of the liturgy and the translation of sacred texts. His letter included specifics concerning the new statutes:

- ICEL was to translate "Roman liturgical texts and books in their integrity." ICEL was to be excluded from the "adaptation, modification or the composition of original texts."
- The "office of executive secretary [was] in need of a careful reconfiguration" to encourage "due accountability" with "a clearer demarcation…from that of the Bishop Members of [ICEL]."
- Paid ICEL employees "should serve *ad tempus*" with renewal procedures for periodic employment.
- Members "currently termed the Advisory Committee or the Secretariat, and their respective collaborators, shall require the *nihil obstat* of this Congregation in order to assume and to maintain their posts…"
- The work of ICEL should be "anonymous and confidential."
- Direct publication of liturgical texts before *recognitio* of the Holy See permitting their use in the Sacred Liturgy was prohibited.
- "The redrafting of the Statutes should be undertaken directly by the Bishop members" of ICEL.

Cardinal Medina's actions signaled a veritable sea change in the usual conduct of liturgical affairs in the Church. Predictably, the president of ICEL, and many other members of the liturgical establishment, felt threatened, and they complained publicly about "Vatican interference" in the business of the bishops.

When the Vatican announced that a new edition of the *Missale Romanum*—the third typical edition—could be expected before the end of the Jubilee Year 2000, and released the new Missal's rubrical introduction, the *Institutio Generalis Missalis Romani* in July, 2000, the reactions from certain liturgical quarters were, again predictably, as energetic as they were negative. Principally because of this heated controversy, the official appearance of the Latin edition of the new Missal was delayed for nearly two years.

But even as ICEL's "thoroughgoing reform" and the controversy over the new Missal and its General Instruction continued unresolved, an event of watershed significance was about to take place—and one with far-reaching implications for Catholic worship.

Liturgiam Authenticam

After three years of preparation, on April 25, 2001, *Liturgiam Authenticam—On the Use of Vernacular Languages in the Publication of the Books of the Roman Liturgy,* was issued by the Congregation for Divine Worship and the Discipline of the Sacraments, after having been expressly approved by Pope John Paul II. It was posted on the Vatican web site the same day. It constituted the Fifth Instruction on the implementation of the Second Vatican Council's liturgical reform, and was obviously one with far-reaching implications for Catholic worship.

Appearing near the end of the massive re-translation and revision of the major liturgical books used by the Catholic Church in English-speaking countries, this authoritative document henceforth set the tone for the translation of new texts and the correction of existing ones:

> The omissions or errors which affect certain existing ver-
> nacular translations ... have impeded the progress of the

> inculturation   that actually should have taken place. In
> fact, it seems necessary to consider anew the true notion
> of liturgical translation in order that the translations of the
> Sacred Liturgy into the vernacular languages may stand
> secure as the authentic voice of the Church of God (LA 7).

Liturgiam Authenticam "seeks to prepare for a new era of liturgical renewal," the document stated, and its concluding words summarize its goal: "It is to be hoped that this new effort will provide stability in the life of the Church, so as to lay a firm foundation for supporting the liturgical life of God's people and bringing about a solid renewal of catechesis" (LA 133).

The appearance of *Liturgiam Authenticam* was considered by many a victory which had been impossible to imagine only a few years earlier. It almost immediately became evident that the quest for authentic liturgy was no longer an impossible dream.

Then, on March 16, 2002, the ICEL Sacramentary was officially rejected, and Cardinal Medina's detailed "observations" on it were published. On March 22, the new Missal was officially promulgated by the pope and presented to the press by Cardinal Medina Estévez. On April 22, the *Vox Clara* commission was appointed by the CDW to oversee liturgical translations in English. On August 1, a new chairman of ICEL was elected, and a new General Secretary appointed, signaling a "thoroughgoing change" in progress.

On October 2, 2002, Cardinal Medina was succeeded as prefect of the CDW by Francis Cardinal Arinze, who would carry on this work. On October 23, Cardinal Arinze criticized ICEL's proposed statutes, which "do not address sufficiently the requirements of the Instruction *Liturgiam Authenticam.*" Then, on Holy Thursday 2003 (April 17), Pope John Paul II issued his 14th and last *Encyclical, Ecclesia de Eucharistia.* Again, the pope saw, more than 20 years after Cardinal Casaroli's address to the Italian liturgy conference, and 15 years after his own letter on the 25th anniversary of *Sacrosanctum Concilium,* the same "shadows" obscuring the truth of the Eucharist:

> Unfortunately, alongside these lights, *there are also
> shadows.* In some places the practice of Eucharistic
> adoration has been almost completely abandoned. In

various parts of the Church abuses have occurred, leading
to confusion with regard to sound faith and Catholic
doctrine concerning this wonderful sacrament. At times
one encounters an extremely reductive understanding of
the Eucharistic mystery. Stripped of its sacrificial meaning,
it is celebrated as if it were simply a fraternal banquet.
Furthermore, the necessity of the ministerial priesthood,
grounded in apostolic succession, is at times obscured and
the sacramental nature of the Eucharist is reduced to its
mere effectiveness as a form of proclamation. This has led
here and there to ecumenical initiatives which, albeit well-
intentioned, indulge in Eucharistic practices contrary to the
discipline by which the Church expresses her faith. How
can we not express profound grief at all this? The Eucharist
is too great a gift to tolerate ambiguity and depreciation.
It is my hope that the present Encyclical Letter will
effectively help to banish the dark clouds of unacceptable
doctrine and practice, so that the Eucharist will continue to
shine forth in all its radiant mystery (EE 10).

On October 17, 2003, ICEL's 40th anniversary, the
organization's new Statutes were approved and sent to bishops,
radically reforming this "mixed commission." Although ICEL was
originally organized in Rome in 1963, during the Second Vatican
Council, by bishops from English-speaking countries who were
attending the Council, in 2003, the Congregation for Divine Worship
and the Discipline of the Sacraments formally established ICEL as
a mixed commission in accordance with the Holy See's Instruction
Liturgiam Authenticam.

On November 22, Pope John Paul II issued a "Chirograph"
on liturgical music and on December 4, the 40th anniversary of
Sacrosanctum Concilium, he released his Apostolic letter on the
Liturgy, *Spiritus et Sponsa.* Then, on February 18, 2004, the first draft
of the new ICEL translation of the Order of Mass was sent to the US
bishops.

The following week, on February 25. 2004, the *Lineamenta*
(or guidelines) for a Synod of Bishops meeting on the Eucharist that
was to take place in October, 2005, were released—and the singular

nature of this Synod session, being devoted to the subject of the Pope's recent encyclical on the Eucharist was stressed in its preface. The *Lineamenta* covered aspects of the encyclical, including the "shadows" Pope John Paul had mentioned:

> The lights which come from the Eucharist as sacrament need to be separated from the shadows which come from human deeds. For example, there are indications in Eucharistic catechesis and practice of an overemphasis on a single aspect, e.g., on the Eucharist as meal, on the baptismal common priesthood, on the sufficiency of a Liturgy of the Word only, and on ecumenical practices at Mass which are contrary to the faith and discipline of the Church.
>
> Ritual practices need to regain a sense of the totality of the mystery of the Eucharist, understood to be: the Word of God proclaimed, the community gathered with a priest who celebrates in *persona Christi,* the rendering of thanks to God the Father for His gifts, the transubstantiation of the bread and wine into the Body and Blood of the Lord, His sacramental presence as a result of the Lord's words of consecration, the offering to the Father of the sacrifice of the Cross and communion with the Body and Blood of the risen Christ (*Lineamenta* 25).

An interesting feature of these *Lineamenta* is its concluding series of 20 questions for study and reflection. Here are some samples:

> **2. *Eucharistic Doctrine and Formation:*** What attempts are being made to transmit the teaching on the Eucharist, whole and entire, to your community and the individual believer? Specifically, how are *The Catechism of the Catholic Church,* nn. 1322-1419, and the Encyclical Letter *Ecclesia de Eucharistia,* being utilized by priests, deacons, consecrated persons and the laity involved in pastoral work? In what way is the formation of faith in the Eucharist being ensured in initial catechesis? In homilies? In the programs of ongoing formation for priests, permanent deacons, and seminarians? Of consecrated persons? Of the laity?
>
> **3. *The Understanding of the Eucharistic Mystery:*** What is the prevailing idea on the Eucharist among priests and the faithful of your community: sacrifice?, memorial of the Paschal Mystery?, the precept of Sunday Mass?, fraternal

meal?, act of adoration? Other...? Practically speaking, is
any one of these ideas prevalent? If so, what is the reason?
4. *The Shadows in the Celebration of the Eucharist:*
In the Encyclical Letter *Ecclesia de Eucharistia* (n. 10)
the Holy Father mentions "shadows" in the celebration
of the Eucharist. What are the negative aspects (abuses,
misunderstandings) existing in Eucharistic worship?
What elements or actions done in practice can obscure the
profound sense of the Eucharistic mystery? What is the
cause of such a disorienting situation for the faithful?
5. *The Eucharistic Celebration and Liturgical Norms:*
In an attempt to be personal and avant-garde, do priests
manifest any attitudes in their celebration of Mass which
are explicitly or implicitly contrary to the liturgical norms
established by the Catholic Church...? In your estimation,
what are the underlying reasons for such behavior? What
elements or actions during the celebration of Holy Mass,
and also in Eucharistic worship outside of Mass, according
to their respective norms and dispositions, should receive
attention so as to highlight the profound sense of this great
Mystery of the faith hidden in the gift of the Eucharist?

On April 23, 2004, the disciplinary Instruction *Redemptionis
Sacramentum* "on certain matters to be observed or to be avoided
regarding the Most Holy Eucharist" was released, in accordance with
Ecclesia de Eucharistia. The document is descriptive and explicit, but
not exhaustive in corrective norms. It states, *inter alia*:

> In order that especially in the celebration of the Sacred
> Liturgy the Church might duly safeguard so great a
> mystery in our own time as well, the Supreme Pontiff has
> mandated that this Congregation for Divine Worship and
> the Discipline of the Sacraments, in collaboration with the
> Congregation for the Doctrine of the Faith, should prepare
> this Instruction treating of certain matters pertaining to the
> discipline of the Sacrament of the Eucharist. Those things
> found in this Instruction are therefore to be read in the
> continuity with the above-mentioned Encyclical Letter,
> *Ecclesia de Eucharistia.*
> It is not at all the intention here to prepare a compendium
> of the norms regarding the Most Holy Eucharist, but

rather, to take up within this Instruction some elements of liturgical norms that have been previously expounded or laid down and even today remain in force in order to assure a deeper appreciation of the liturgical norms; to establish certain norms by which those earlier ones are explained and complemented; and also to set forth for Bishops, as well as for Priests, Deacons and all the lay Christian faithful, how each should carry them out in accordance with his own responsibilities and the means at his disposal (RS 2).

Redemptionis Sacramentum's most unusual directive is found in its final chapter, "Remedies," where it highlights the responsibility of every Catholic, whether clergy or lay, to correct liturgical abuses. In a section titled "Complaints Regarding Abuses in Liturgical Matters," we read that:

(183) In an altogether particular manner, let everyone do all that is in their power to ensure that the Most Holy Sacrament of the Eucharist will be protected from any and every irreverence or distortion and that all abuses be thoroughly corrected. This is a most serious duty incumbent upon each and every one, and all are bound to carry it out without any favoritism.

(184) Any Catholic, whether Priest or Deacon or lay member of Christ's faithful, has the right to lodge a complaint regarding a liturgical abuse to the diocesan Bishop or the competent Ordinary equivalent to him in law, or to the Apostolic See on account of the primacy of the Roman Pontiff. It is fitting, however, insofar as possible, that the report or complaint be submitted first to the diocesan Bishop. This is naturally to be done in truth and charity.

On June 10, 2004, on the Solemnity of Corpus Christi, Pope John Paul announced the "Year of the Eucharist," October 2004-2005; and, in launching this observance, he issued his apostolic letter, *Mane Nobiscum Domine* ("Stay with us, Lord") on October 7, which not only called for increased attention to the celebration of Mass, but urged, in particular, Eucharistic Adoration.

During this year *Eucharistic* adoration outside Mass should become a particular commitment for individual parish and

religious communities. Let us take the time to kneel before
Jesus present in the Eucharist, in order to make reparation
by our faith and love for the acts of carelessness and neglect,
and even the insults which our Savior must endure in many
parts of the world. Let us deepen through adoration our
personal and communal contemplation, drawing upon aids
to prayer inspired by the word of God and the experience
of so many mystics, old and new (MND 18).

The Church's observance of the Year of the Eucharist was
begun by one pope, John Paul II, and concluded by another pope,
Benedict XVI. Today, nearly a year after its conclusion, we are
awaiting the final report of that Synod on the Eucharist.

In June of this year, 2006, Pope Benedict said he was eager to
review the final report of the *"relators"* of the Synod session. He may
follow the usual practice of his predecessor and issue an Apostolic
Letter on the subject of the Eucharist reflecting the Synod fathers'
conclusions, though this is not obligatory. Some have speculated that
he may include in such a letter that the "old Mass" may be freely
celebrated by any priest who chooses to do so—a "universal indult,"
as some call it. I would not care to speculate on this. In an address
in 1998 on the 10th anniversary of *Ecclesia Dei,* Cardinal Ratzinger
said:

> The authority of the Church can define and limit the usage
> of rites in different historical circumstances. But the
> Church never purely and simply prohibits them. And so the
> Council did ordain a reform of the liturgical books, but it
> did not forbid the previous books.[17]

He also observed, in this same 1998 speech, that although
"creativity" with the new *Ordo Missae* "has often gone too far, there
is often a greater difference between liturgies celebrated in different
places according to the new books than there is between an old liturgy
and a new liturgy when both are celebrated as they ought to be, in
accordance with the prescribed liturgical texts." Further, he stressed,
"An average Christian without special liturgical training finds it hard to
distinguish between a Mass sung in Latin according to the old Missal
and a Mass sung in Latin according to the new Missal." He suggested
that the "aversions" to one or the other "are so great because the two

forms of celebration are thought to reflect two different spiritual attitudes, two different ways of perceiving the Church and the whole of Christian life."

The Council did not represent a rupture, but expressed *continuity* with the Church's history: "There is no 'pre-' or 'post-' conciliar Church," the future Pope Benedict said. "There is but one, unique Church that walks the path toward the Lord..."[18]

This past June, following his meeting with the committee of "*relators*" who presented their summary of the Synod on the Eucharist's final Propositions, Pope Benedict said that he hopes "that I shall soon see and be able myself to learn from this text, which can then be published for the benefit of the whole Church that is eagerly expecting it....And this text which is being drafted will be one such intervention to nourish the People of God with the food of the truth, to help them grow in truth and especially to make known the mystery of the Eucharist and invite them to an intense Eucharistic life." He also commented that after his predecessor's *Ecclesia de Eucharistia*, and *Mane Nobiscum Domine*, "what more can be said"?

More than four decades have passed since the first words of the Second Vatican Council on the subject of the liturgy appeared:

> This Sacred Council has several aims in view: it desires to impart an ever increasing vigor to the Christian life of the faithful; to adapt more suitably to the needs of our own times those institutions which are subject to change; to foster whatever can promote union among all who believe in Christ; to strengthen whatever can help to call the whole of mankind into the household of the Church. The Council therefore sees particularly cogent reasons for undertaking the reform and promotion of the Liturgy (SC 1).

Forty years is a long time—and calls to mind biblical images. Much remains to be done before the authentic renewal of the sacred Liturgy is accomplished. And the road will not be easy. There is still opposition to authentic liturgical reform on several fronts, and this will continue. The Church still suffers from internal divisions, and her mission in our time has been damaged by scandals as well as loss of faith. The "spirit of the age" is hostile to the Church and rejects her fundamental moral teachings and doctrine, as well as her authority to teach. No one understands this more acutely than Pope Benedict XVI, and no one has written more incisively about it, as his first encyclical, *Deus Caritas Est*, further revealed.

Yet, despite the problems, the compass for the recovery of the sacred dimension of the Liturgy has now been firmly set. And our goal is now more clearly in view. We must work to "banish the dark clouds of unacceptable doctrine and practice, so that the Eucharist will continue to shine forth in all its radiant mystery," as Pope John Paul II said in *Ecclesia de Eucharistia.*

We do not know exactly how to "banish the dark clouds," which often appear impenetrable. But we do know the Source of the strength and courage we will need for this task. It is Jesus Christ, "the same yesterday and today and forever" (Heb 13:8). And we know where to find His answer. As Pope Benedict wrote in his book, *God is Near Us*:

> The Eucharist is God as an answer, as an answering presence. Now the initiative no longer lies with us, in the God/man relationship, but with Him. …Indeed, it is now not just two-way, but all-inclusive: whenever we pray in the Eucharistic presence, we are never alone. Then the whole of the Church, which celebrates the Eucharist, is praying with us".[19]

So let us go forth, then, and with confidence, as is recorded in the Letter to the Hebrews:

> Therefore let us go forth to Him outside the camp, bearing abuse for Him. For here we have no lasting city, but we seek the city which is to come. Through Him, then, let us continually offer up a sacrifice of praise to God, that is, the fruit of lips that acknowledge His name" (Heb 13:3,15).

Helen Hull Hitchcock is the founding director (in 1984) of the lay association Women for Faith and Family (WFF) and she continues in that capacity today. She is also the editor of the WFF journal, Voices. Since 1995 she has also been the editor of the *Adoremus Bulletin,* the publication of the Adoremus Society for the Renewal of the Sacred Liturgy, of which she is a co-founder. In 1992, she edited the volume entitled *The Politics of Prayer: Feminist Language and the Worship of God* (Ignatius Press). She has been a regular columnist for both Crisis magazine and *The National Catholic Register*, and she has also published articles in other publications such as *Touchstone* and *The Catholic World Report.*

Mrs. Hitchcock is a native of Kansas, and she holds an AB in Art History and English from the University of Kansas. She also did post-graduate work in philosophy at the University of California in Berkeley. She is currently a member of the board of directors of EWTN and has appeared on its "Journey Home" show. Formerly she was a member of the board of directors of the Fellowship of Catholic Scholars and she received the FCS Cardinal O'Boyle Award in 2004. She is married to James Hitchcock, and they are the parents of four daughters and are now grandparents as well. With her husband, she chaired the program committee for this year's FCS convention on *Sacrosanctum Concilium.*

Endnotes

[1]ICET was dissolved in 1975 after the publication of a revised edition of *Prayers We Have In Common,* but it was succeeded in 1985 by the English Language Liturgical Commission (ELLC), organized for the same purpose, including Anglican, Lutheran, Methodist, Reformed (Presbyterian), Catholic, and United Church of Christ members, and was open to the Orthodox and other Eastern churches as well as "Free Church" groups.

[2]Joseph Cardinal Ratzinger, "Ten Years after the Publication of *Ecclesia Dei*" (address given in Rome, October 24, 1998, translated from original French by Father Ignatius Harrison, and accessible online http://www.unavoce.org/tenyears.htm).

[3]"The Advisory Committee recognizes the necessity in all future translations and revisions to avoid words which ignore the place of women in the Christian community altogether or which seem to relegate women to a secondary role" (Minutes of the Advisory Committee Meeting, August 1975). Quoted in "Statement: The Problem of Exclusive Language with Regard to Women," p. 63ff, in ICEL, *Eucharistic Prayers,* 1980. This "Green Book" was issued by ICEL "for study and comment by the Bishops of the Member and Associate Member Countries of the International Commission on English in the Liturgy." This "Green Book" contained draft revisions of the Eucharistic Prayers in order to "eliminate from these liturgical texts anything that has been judged to be exclusive or exclusionary...that may be considered discriminatory to women" (p 3).

[4]*The Bishops Committee on the Liturgy Newsletter* (BCL Newsletter), December 1981 (Vol XVII) announced that a letter dated November 17, 1981, from Archbishop Pio Laghi to the U.S. bishops informed them that the Holy Father "approved the proposal" for this change, which took effect immediately.

[5]McManus, Frederick R., Editor. *Thirty Years of Liturgical Renewal— Statements of the Bishops' Committee on the Liturgy.* Washington, DC.: Secretariat, Bishops' Committee on the Liturgy, NCCB. July, 1987, p. 250.

[6]National Conference of Catholic Bishops, AGENDA REPORT, November, 1991, report of the NCCB Committee on the Liturgy, p. 27.

[7]Cardinal Agostino Casaroli, Letter dated August 20, 1981, to mark the 32nd National Liturgical Week sponsored by the Center for Liturgical Action, Creme, Italy. (Published in *BCL Newsletter,* August-September 1981, Vol. XVII.).

[8]This and numerous other re-translation projects, major and minor, approved by the bishops or in progress, and principles governing the process, are described in the AGENDA REPORT, Documentation for General Meeting of the NCCB, November 11-14, 1991; Action Items 2-4, reports by the Liturgy Committee (pp. 1-11, 228-234; 238-240), and in Information Items, p. 25-34.
Also in the AGENDA REPORT (Action Items pp. 252-256) is the report of the Committee on Pastoral Practices on granting of imprimaturs in the name of the NCCB by a small internal committee. Other less sweeping revisions were planned as part of the "inculturation" process for "Native Americans" and other minority groups.

[9]AGENDA REPORT, p. 233, 234 - emphasis added.

[10]AGENDA REPORT - Action Items, p 11. During the NCCB meeting, the Lectionary for Masses with Children became known in the press-room as the "Sesame Street Bible" or the "Away-in-a-Feedbox" translation, referring in particular to the

translation of "manger" as "feedbox." Despite the energetic defense of "feedbox" by the chairmen of the bishops' committees on Liturgy and Pastoral Practices, the bishops voted to change the word back to "manger." This was the only emendation the bishops sought before granting their approval to the entire text.

[11]*Ibid.* p. 238.

[12]AGENDA REPORT - Information Items, p 113. "ICEL's income is from the liturgical texts that it prepares and licenses publishers to produce after the authorization of the conferences. Present indications are that ICEL's financial condition will be difficult over the next few years, beginning particularly in 1993. This situation results from the high costs of the Missal revision project, which will have taken twelve years from the initial consultation phase to the presentation to the conferences, and from a decline in overall revenues from the earlier liturgical books prepared by ICEL. More recent books, such as the *Order of Christian Funerals, the Rite of Christian Initiation of Adults, the Book of Blessings,* and the *Ceremonial of Bishops,* while providing some revenue, have brought only a small infusion of funds. In some cases the monies spent in preparing these texts have yet to be recouped and realistically may never be, given the many costs involved in preparing liturgical books. The declining financial situation will likely continue until the beginning of 1997, when new income is expected from the revised Missal."

[13]Pope John Paul II, Address to the bishops of California, Nevada and Hawaii, December 4, 1993; published in *L'Osservatore Romano* December 15, 1993.

[14]In the United States, for example, both the *Adoremus*- Society for the Renewal of the Sacred Liturgy and the Society for Catholic Liturgy were organized in 1995, and the following year "The Oxford Declaration" was issued by the Society for Catholic Culture in England. Credo, an organization of priests committed to improved translations, was formed in 1992, and Women for Faith & Family, organized in 1984 to support Church teachings, had consistently opposed the influence of feminist theology on language and liturgy.

[15]Quoted from Catholic News Service report, June 13, 1996.

[16]Letter of Cardinal Medina to Bishop Maurice Taylor, October 26, 1999.

[17]"Ten Years after the Publication of *Ecclesia Dei* (Address given in Rome, October 24, 1998, translated from original French by Fr. Ignatius Harrison, and accessible online http://www.unavoce.org/tenyears.htm).

[18]Joseph Cardinal Ratzinger with Vittorio Messori The Ratzinger Report, San Francisco: Ignatius 1985, p 35.

[19]*God Is Near Us*, San Francisco: Ignatius Press, 2001, p 90.

XI.

Session V
Ecclesia de Eucharistia –
Litugy and Mission

The Liturgy and Social Justice
Rev. Msgr. Stewart Swetland

When first conceived, this paper was intended to be an exposition on the relationship between the rubrics of the Mass and the duty of the priest celebrant and liturgical planners to offer the people of God the Mass as the Church intends for it to be celebrated. In other words, this essay was intended to be a diatribe against the *injustices* done to the people of God by those who would—because of their own subjective notions of what is or is not "just"—arbitrarily change the words, order, and meaning of our liturgical prayer to suit their own ideologies. As a convert, I was particularly sensitive to this as a layman having suffered through numerous Masses, baptisms, and weddings where the priest would inflict upon us the most egregious liturgical abuses.

Of the many, many examples of these abuses that could be given (after all, I served in the Navy in a diocese where priests were known for such outrages as driving a Volkswagen up the aisle on Palm Sunday or having a crane lift him out of the sanctuary at the end of Mass on Ascension Thursdays), one must suffice. In my first year of seminary, a priest-celebrant instructed the lector to refrain from reading the part of the first reading where Paul told the Church of Thessalonica that "anyone who would not work should not eat."[1] He commanded this of the seminarian lector because this verse was not, according to this priest, "compatible with Catholic Social Teaching"! You can imagine how such creative "editing" of sacred Scripture played with this young convert's understanding of the place of Biblical Truth within Catholic Tradition.

In particular, this essay was meant to examine and counter the false notion that the local congregation and main celebrant had the right and power to such liturgical creativity based on an appeal to "justice" or "social justice." It seemed that those most bent on promoting the *injustice* of liturgical abuses onto the people of God were just those who would must advocate the need to live and practice a particular version of the Church's social teaching.

In other words, they would do something patently *unjust* (arbitrarily changing the rubrics and words of the Church's liturgy) in the name of eliminating perceived "injustices." This practice was so common that many parishioners came to associate advocacy for "social justice" with such abuses and easily dismissed both. As the one who first formed in me the virtue of justice (my mother) taught, two wrongs do not make a right.

While still holding that it is unjust to afflict God's people with such liturgical abuses, after much study and reflection on the relationship between social justice and liturgy, it is fitting and right that this relatively minor concern be placed in the broader context of the rich history and tradition of the way that the commitment and practice of the virtue of justice and the authentic and fruitful celebration of the liturgy interpenetrate each other.

This can best be done, it would seem, by examining three aspects of the relationship between social justice and liturgy. These are: the Liturgy as the Justice of God; the Liturgy and Our Response to God's Justice; and the Obligation of Justice in the Liturgy.

The Liturgy as the Justice of God

What does Social Justice have to do with liturgy? I have been asked this question by numerous Catholics when I mention my research in this area. Some would see a vague relationship, commenting on the need to pray if one would "do justice," or talk of the special liturgical celebrations which emphasized the social question (like the Mass for Peace and Justice or a Lenten Communal Penance service). But most seem to imply, by the way they ask the question, that the obvious answer was little or nothing. They think like Tertullian when he asked, rhetorically, "What does Athens have to do with Jerusalem?" that the question answers itself.

And much of the liturgical theology written in the early post-Vatican II era would seem to confirm this assumption. For example, very little is mentioned in the *New Catholic Encyclopedia*'s almost one hundred pages on Liturgy, Liturgical Art, Liturgical Reform, etc., even remotely about social justice, except for a brief section about the communal aspect of liturgy in the articles about Liturgy, Liturgical Reforms, and Liturgical Participation.[2] Even these, though, are "balanced" by being placed in the context where the liturgy is presented as both hierarchical and communal.[3] Likewise, the fifty pages of articles related to social justice, social work, and Catholic social action do not make any references to the Church's liturgical life.[4] Similarly, one finds no entries in the index of the massive volume *Documents on the Liturgy 1963-1979: Conciliar, Papal, and Curial Texts* for justice, social justice, solidarity, etc.[5] You also will not find any such discussion in major reference works and textbooks on the Liturgy such as *The Study of Liturgy*[6] and *Handbook for Liturgical Studies: Introduction to the Liturgy.*[7]

This seeming lack of concern by scholarly and magisterial works on the relationship between liturgy and social justice was commented on by Fr. J. Bryan Hehir as early as 1979. Speaking at the Eighth Annual Notre Dame Conference on Pastoral Liturgy, he stated that this lack of integration was mainly caused by the various disciplines' great need to assimilate the advances associated with Vatican II in their own area. What had not happened, according to Father Hehir, was a full integration of faith and life, liturgy and social justice work alluded to in the Conciliar Text.

This is more than somewhat surprising given the history of the relationship between liturgical reform and social justice. What is striking as one studies the tremendous works of the Liturgical Movement in the early to mid-Twentieth Century is how passionate most (if not all) of those great reformers were in working for a more just social order. The writings of Henri de Lubac, Dom Odo Casel, Karl Adam, Pius Parsch, Louis Bouyer, Josef Jungman, Romano Guardini,

Karl Rahner, and many others led to and built upon the advances in liturgical renewal and the Church's social doctrine embodied in the pontificates of St. Pius X, Pius XI, and Pius XII.[8] This is particularly true of the Liturgical Movement in the United States. One thinks of such giants as Fr. Virgil Michel, O.S.B., of Collegeville and Msgr. Reynold Hillenbrand of Chicago. These men both believed in the need for a social regeneration. Both believed that this would be possible only if there was a renewed Christian Spirit in the men and women of society. And this would only be possible if there was a genuine renewal of the liturgy. This is how Msgr. Hillenbrand's life's work was recently summarized:

> He was a leading figure in the liturgical and social action movement in the United States during the 1930s and worked to promote active, intelligent, and informed participation in the Church's liturgy. He believed that a reconstruction of society would occur as a result of the renewal of the Christian spirit, whose source and center is the liturgy. Hillenbrand taught that, since the ultimate purpose of Catholic action is to Christianize society, the renewal of the liturgy must undoubtedly play the key role in achieving this goal.[9]

Fr. Virgil Michel wrote his own summary of the relationship between social reform and the liturgy by way of a syllogism:

> Pius X tells us that the liturgy is the indispensable source of the true Christian spirit; Pius XI says that the true Christian spirit is indispensable for social regeneration. Hence the conclusion. The liturgy is the indispensable basis of Christian social regeneration.[10]

These men typified the strong correlation between the early Liturgical Movement and the desire among many Catholics for authentic social reform.

Fr. Hehir believes that the work of the great theologians of the Liturgical Movement culminated in the reforms of the Second Vatican Council. If this is true (and I believe that it is), it makes the relative silence about the relationship between social justice and the liturgy for the roughly 15-20 years (a biblical generation!) after the Council all the more striking. But academics, like nature, hate a vacuum. The absence of such works in the early post-Conciliar period has been filled by a bevy of books and conferences, articles, etc., on the subject. However, unlike their predecessors, many of these books and articles are not grounded in the Church's tradition. In fact, many of them take that very tradition to task for perceived slights and injustices. Completely lost is the idea that the Church's liturgy and sacraments are something that we first and primarily receive from God, not something we invent or do on our own.

A prime example of this new type of text is Megan McKenna's book *Rites of Justice: The Sacraments and Liturgy as Ethical Imperatives.*[11] Much in this work is a challenge to take seriously the communal and ethical demands that following Christ places on the believer. But her understanding of the sacramental life and liturgy has been almost completely separated from the Catholic tradition from which she states that she is writing.

A comparison of McKenna to the Council of Trent is illuminating. First, two paragraphs from McKenna discussing the sacraments of marriage and orders:

> Although baptism initiates us into the church and gives us the opportunity if not the recourse to all the sacraments that belong to all the people of God, not all adults receive marriage or orders—and one usually precludes the other. A growing number of adults in the church are excluded from both at a time when adult Christians need the support, grace, and celebration of their lifestyles within the church and the world.
>
> In order to deal with some of these theological inconsistencies, I approach marriage and orders as sacraments of lifestyle within the Christian community. In the following chapters I will offer some suggestions for altering the celebration of these sacraments and how and who participates in them, as well as suggesting new sacraments. Sacraments are, after all, the heritage of Christians and can be claimed and re-created according to need. In these chapters I will deal with the reality of ministry, apart from the sacrament of orders, as charism,

and with both single and religious commitments within the church that need to be sacramentalized. I deliberately avoid dealing with marriage primarily in regard to its more institutionalized demands as found in canon law and/or the issues of sexuality; I prefer the context of friendship, love, and faithfulness. I suggest further that all adult Christians be able to receive this sacrament in the context of friendship with one to whom they are faithful, no matter the choice of their vocation within the church. The sacraments of the friends of God includes *all* expressions of faithful love in the community of believers.[12]

Here is the infallible decree of the seventh session of the Council of Trent:

For the completion of the salutary doctrine on justification, which was promulgated with the unanimous consent of the Fathers in the last session, it has seemed proper to deal with the most holy sacraments of the Church, through which all true justice either begins, or being begun, is increased, or being lost is restored.

Canon 1. If anyone says that the sacraments of the New Law were not instituted by our Lord Jesus Christ, or that there are more or less than seven, namely, baptism, confirmation, Eucharist, penance, extreme unction, orders and matrimony, or that any one of these seven is not truly and intrinsically a sacrament, let him be anathema.[13]

What is of particular interest is how McKenna, in the name of inclusivity, has referred to these sacraments as "sacraments of Christian lifestyle." In contrast, the *Catechism of the Catholic Church* refers to them as "sacraments at the service of communion" and states at paragraph 1534:

Two other sacraments, Holy Orders and Matrimony, are directed towards the salvation of others; if they contribute as well to personal salvation, it is through service to others that they do so. They confer a particular mission in the Church and serve to build up the People of God.

Here one sees a true Christian spirit of justice as service to others and a building of communion. Other texts have a similar bent. Many of them deal with the perceived "injustice" of continuing the tradition of ordaining only men to the priesthood. For example, Rosemary Haughton, in a paper entitled, "The Spirituality of Social Justice," ironically given at a symposium in honor of Virgil Michel, writes that the "issue of sexism" must be of primary concern for the Church:

> What I am suggesting is that a spirituality of social justice
> has to be concerned, probably before anything else, with
> the issue of sexism, of the normative patriarchal fear of the
> feminine and the consequent oppression and abuse of women.
> Unless we are working at the roots of this injustice, we will
> never release the power of the spirit in our churches.[14]

Another voice raising similar concerns is Sr. Frances B. O'Connor, C.S.C. of Holy Cross and Notre Dame. O'Connor writes that "the Church must give witness to justice,"[15] but does not do so because of its failure to include women among the ordained. She also calls for an end to all "sexist" language and the omission of texts deemed offensive to women.[16] O'Connor believes that necessary change will only come when liturgists get "angry":

> Liturgists need to develop a just and holy anger. Thomas
> Aquinas said it is morally wrong not to be angry when you
> encounter a situation of injustice. What is more unjust than
> to deprive women of full participation in the liturgy?[17]

Although I have focused on women scholars, to be fair, male theologians such as Fr. Keenan Osborne, O.F.M., Fr. John Wijngaards, Msgr. Jack Egan, and Fr. Michael Crosby could just as easily be cited saying similar things, at least when it comes to the ordination of women.

What all of these recent writings share is the belief that the sacramental life is open to change in these or other ways because it is mainly what *we* do. But, in fact, this is not true. Liturgy is mainly about what God is doing *pro nobis* (for us). Even if these theologians accept this truth in theory, their proposed practice betrays a different sentiment. What must be retrieved is an understanding of the liturgy as God's work for us.

Liturgy as the Display of God's Justice

In the seventh session of the Council of Trent quoted above, one finds the Council Fathers teaching that all true justice begins, increases, or is restored via the sacraments. Of course, here the Council is mainly referring to the justice of justification—man's being made right with or righteous before God. But there is another sense in which their statement is true. The liturgy is "the place where God's justice is made manifest—displayed," in the words of Fr. Robert Barron.

Prof. Mark Searle of Notre Dame made this point explicitly: "The liturgy celebrates the justice of God himself, as revealed by him in history, recorded in the Scriptures, and proclaimed in the assembly of the faithful."[18] Fr. Barron reminds us how it is essential to see the liturgy as an icon of God's activity and our response:

> In this essay I would like to explore a basic implication of the *lex orandi lex credendi* principle. I will endeavor to show that the liturgy is not only an act of worship, but also an iconic display of the uniquely Christian understanding of both God and human society. More precisely, it is a showing forth of the *ordo* of non-violent love that is the Trinity and of the *ordo* of a properly functioning humanity. As such, I will argue, the liturgy is also a source of world transformation, the catalyst by which the Trinitarian *communio* impresses itself on a world rendered dysfunctional through sin and violence.[19]

Searle and Barron have both rediscovered an important aspect of liturgy well-known to the Fathers of the Church and the early pioneers of the Liturgical Movement, but seemingly "forgotten" by many modern liturgists.

As *Gaudium et Spes* 22 teaches, a proper understanding of both God and man is discovered in the person of Jesus Christ. Christ reveals man to man and makes his divine vocation clear. Thus, in a particular way, as Barron demonstrates, humanity discovers who God is and who we can be in the Paschal Mystery of Jesus Christ.[20] Just what does his life, death, and resurrection reveal? God's mercy and our sinfulness. Jesus came into the world to reveal to the world the love of the Father. In our sinful world, that love takes the particular form of mercy. But we reject Jesus' witness to love—a love that Barron describes as "inclusive," "healing," "forgiving," and "non-violent"—and put him to death. We are all complicit in his death. But the Father vindicates Jesus' faithfulness by demonstrating convincingly that death, sin, and Satan cannot prevail over love by raising Jesus from the dead. A new age has dawned in the resurrection—an age where God's way of love has overcome the powers and principalities opposed to it. By our union with Jesus we can share in this new "way," which is nothing more or less than the very life of God himself. We can live in union with the *communio* of the Triune God. We can do this in a supreme way in the liturgy of the Church. Barron writes:

> It is, in the very structure of its life, the icon of the Paschal Mystery, of the non-violent God, and its purpose is, frankly, subversive. It is meant, through a kind of spiritual osmosis, to transform the City of Man from within, undermining its structures of violence and replacing them with structures of love. Its weapons are prayer, martyrdom, the witness of the saints, forgiveness, preaching and, above all, the liturgy. If the church is the icon of God's forgiving love, then the liturgy, source and summit of the church's life, is the icon of icons. The liturgy is an artistic display of the deepest truth about ourselves and about God, a "place" in which the new being, the City of God, is concretely realized.[21]

Barron's work displays how the liturgy properly celebrated fulfills its iconic function. For example, he reminds the reader of the important fact, all too often overlooked, of just how radical our assemblies are. They are in themselves an icon of *communio*. Barron tells the story of Christopher Dawson's conversion and his parents' opposition. After Dawson tried to show his parents the reasonableness of the Catholic faith, his mother was forced to say, "I'm not so much concerned about their theology; it's just that you'll be worshipping with the help!" Dorothy Day used to define the Church as "here comes everyone." In my own experience, at no time or place will you find such true diversity in America than at most Catholic Churches on Sunday.

We begin our celebration with the Sign of the Cross. Here is how Barron describes this symbol:

> After the community has gathered and has solidified its communion through song, the liturgy proper begins with

the Sign of the Cross. This gesture, of course, places the whole Mass under the control of the Paschal Mystery. More precisely, it signals the "opening up" of the divine persons that is the ground for our participation in the divine life. If God were monolithically one, we would always relate extrinsically to him, praying, supplicating, worshipping from the outside. But the God of Christians is not a monolith; he is a *communio* of love between differentiated persons. And we, through the dying and rising of Jesus, have been invited into the broken heart of God, into the space between the Father and the Son which is the Holy Spirit. This means that we pray, not from outside the divine, but from within God's own life, our *communio* nestling in the incomprehensibility more intense *communio* of the Trinity. Thus the simple gesture of the Sign of the Cross shows the deepest ground for our challenge to the injustice of the City of Man.[22]

Barron's article continues by describing the entire Mass in this way.

The key to all this, and the reason that it is worth describing in detail, is that in the liturgy, the justice of God is made clear. God's answer to sin and suffering is on display. We are allowed and invited to participate in His justice. Then having joined with Him and having been transformed by the Holy Spirit to be made more into the image of Christ, we are sent forth to transform our world in accordance with the justice of God. Here is how Searle describes this process:

In every generation some people are called by name consciously to serve this Kingdom and its justice as revealed in Jesus. They are called Christians, and together, as a new humanity, they have the unenviable responsibility of representing the hope of a higher justice and working for its realization. It is not that the Kingdom and justice of God are to be found only among them, but they are called and commissioned in its service. The form in which they received that commission is the ritual known as baptism, in which they are called to surrender themselves to the god who revealed himself in Jesus and whom they acknowledge as the Creator of the world and the Lord of history. These disciples of Jesus, who die to the man-made and demonically disjointed world of their times, begin to live according to a new order and according to a new principle: the Spirit of God who enables them to do the works of God.[23]

The liturgy is first and foremost God's work of justice that we participate in through His grace.

The Liturgy and Our Response to God's Justice

Obviously, from what has been said above, our first response to God's justice, initiated by Him, is to receive the gift with gratitude. This priority of receptivity is central to social justice. Before we can act, we must first receive. "Without Me you can do nothing," as Jesus teaches us in the Gospel of John (John 15:5).

Having received everything from him as gift, our next response is that of praise, gratitude, and thanksgiving. As we pray in the liturgy: "It is right to give Him thanks and praise." As many commentators point out, St. Thomas made the virtue of religion (whereby we render to God the honor we owe him) allied to the virtue of justice. It is indeed right and good to give God thanks and praise.

After honoring God with our gratitude, thanks, and praise, we honor Him by our lives of living service. It begins by living our lives to the fullest in accord with our vocation. As St. Irenaeus taught: "The glory of God is man fully alive." And this faithfulness is best achieved through our total gift of self to others in service. "The greatest among you must serve the rest" (Mt 20:27).

At the close of every liturgy, we are blessed and sent forth. This sending forth is meant to be seen in terms of our *missio*—our mission. By our baptisms, all of us have a share in the one mission of Jesus Christ. His mission was to reveal to the world the love of the Father. This love as we saw above is an inclusive, healing, merciful, and non-violent love (as long as we interpret non-violent as inclusive of condemning hypocrisy and chasing money-changers out of the temple). Each of us will make manifest this type of love differently in accordance with our particular vocation in life. In Sacred Scripture, encounters with the Risen Lord inevitably led to a mission ("Go, tell my brothers"; "feed my sheep"; "whose sins you forgive are forgiven"; "Go into all the world," etc.) So our encounter today with the power of the Risen Lord should lead to mission.

Justice in the Liturgy

Our love and service towards others begins in the liturgy itself. Because the assembly is to be the community of persons in friendship with God and through God with each other (thus, to be truly an icon of the Kingdom), then it is necessary that the communion of the Church really reflects the communion of the Kingdom. Thus, Jesus teaches us the importance of being reconciled to our brothers before we offer sacrifice to God: "If you bring your gift to the altar and there recall that your brother has anything against you, leave your gift at the altar, go first to be reconciled with your brother, and then come and offer your gift" (Mt 5:23-24). Similarly, St. Paul admonishes the Church at Corinth for their lack of charity, concern, and justice towards one another in their Eucharistic assembly:

> What I now have to say is not said in praise, because your meetings are not profitable but harmful. First of all, I hear that when you gather for a meeting, there are divisions among you, and I am inclined to believe it. There may even have to be factions among you for the tried and true to stand out clearly. When you assemble it is not to eat the Lord's Supper, for everyone is in haste to eat his own supper. One person goes hungry while another gets drunk. Do you not have homes where you can eat and drink? Would you show contempt for the church of God, and embarrass those who have nothing? What can I say to you? Shall I praise you? Certainly not in this matter![24]

The *communio* of the praying assembly should be model for our efforts to sanctify the world and to help build the Kingdom.

Thus, our commitment to justice and service should be clearly seen in the liturgy. This is the reason that their priest (or some assembly of liturgists or liturgy committee members) ought not to impose on the people of God liturgies that are not in accordance with the rubrics of the Church. This is, pure and simple, an injustice imposed on God's people. The Council teaches this clearly in *Sacrosanctum Concilium,*

22: "Therefore, no other person, not even a priest, may add, remove, or change anything in the liturgy on his own authority." This seems quite clear but yet the clericalism and arrogance of some clergy (and some liturgists) in this area knows no bounds.

This being said, all of us in the Church must recognize that there will always be disagreements and differences about the language and style of our liturgies. Fortunately, the Church allows a relatively wide latitude in our choices and approaches. But we ought to stay within those approved texts and prayers. Cardinal Francis George reminds us that when it comes to liturgy, there are no small changes. This is because one is dealing with the place, time, and language of intimacy of encounter. Thus, sensitivities will always be high.

There is one more area of justice in the liturgy that must be discussed. It is an issue where I believe much serious theological debate should take place. We all desire our churches to be beautiful. We all wish for the ornamentation, the vessels, the vestments, the artwork, etc., that are so much a part of our liturgies to be among the best that we have to offer. This being said, when is enough, enough? What is "too much" when it comes to Church decorations and costs? We have a direct challenge from John Paul II in this regard when he wrote in *Sollicitudo Rei Socialis* 31:

> Thus, part of the *teaching* and most ancient *practice* of the Church is her conviction that she is obliged by her vocation—she herself, her ministers and each of her members—to relieve the misery of the suffering, both far and near, not only out of her "abundance" but also out of her "necessities." Faced by cases of need, one cannot ignore them in favor of superfluous church ornaments and costly furnishings for divine worship; on the contrary, it could be obligatory to sell these goods in order to provide food, drink, clothing, and shelter for those who lack these things.

In this, John Paul II was following in the footsteps of a great Church Father of the East and Doctor of the Church, St. John Chrysostom, who wrote

> Do you want to honor Christ's body? Then do not scorn him in his nakedness, do not honor him here in the church

with silken garments while neglecting him outside where
he is cold and naked...Give him the honor prescribed in
his law by giving your riches to the poor. For God does not
want golden vessels but golden hearts.

Now, in saying this, I am not forbidding you to make such
gifts; I am demanding that along with such gifts and before
them you give alms...Of what use is it to weigh down
Christ's table with golden cups, when he himself is dying
of hunger? First, fill him when he is hungry; then use the
means you have left to adorn his table.[25]

Both of these quotations speak of the priority of persons over
things—of seeing and serving Christ in our brother and sister in need.
But much thought and reflection must go into how we find the proper
balance. One truth I do know from my own pastoral experience: the
poor in a particular way desire their churches to be beautiful and well-
kept.

Conclusion

The liturgy makes present for us the justice of God. The liturgy
challenges us to receive God's merciful love with praise and gratitude.
The liturgy empowers us and transforms us and sends us forth into
the world to carry on the mission of Jesus. The liturgy demands of
us a just and fitting celebration of God's love. Ultimately, the liturgy
allows us to enter into adoration of God which leads to mission. Pope
Benedict XVI taught this clearly to the Curia with his first Christmas
greetings delivered December 22, 2005:

Indeed, we do not merely receive something in the
Eucharist. It is the encounter and unification of persons.
The person, however, who comes to meet us and desires to
unite himself to us is the Son of God. Such unification can
only be brought about by means of adoration. Receiving
the Eucharist means adoring the One whom we receive.
Precisely in this way and only in this way do we become
one with him. Therefore, the development of Eucharistic
adoration, as it took shape during the Middle Ages, was
the most consistent consequence of the Eucharistic
mystery itself: Only in adoration can profound and true
acceptance develop. And it is precisely this personal act of

encounter with the Lord that develops the social mission which is contained in the Eucharist and desires to break down barriers, not only the barriers between the Lord and us but also and above all those that separate us from one another.[26]

All too often the barriers that need breaking down are those between advocates of social justice and advocates of liturgical renewal. In fact, as Benedict makes clear, the Catholic resolution is found in the Eucharist, where both our hunger and thirst for righteousness and for the Lord is satiated. In the liturgy, the justice of God is made manifest and service and worship become one.

Monsignor Stuart W. Swetland was ordained a priest in 1991 for the diocese of Peoria, Illinois. He is a former naval officer and received his undergraduate degree in physics from the United States Naval Academy in Annapolis. Elected a Rhodes Scholar in 1981, he entered the Catholic Church while he was studying at Oxford University. He has a B.A. and M.A. in politics, philosophy, and economics from Oxford, an M.Div. and M.A. from St. Mary's Seminary, and an S.T.L. and S.T.D. from the pontifical Lateran University where he studied at the John Paul II Institute in Washington, D.C.

Msgr. Swetland currently serves as the Director of Homiletics and Pre-Theology at Mount St. Mary's Seminary in Emmitsburg, Maryland. He also currently serves as a theological advisor to the Catholic Conference of Illinois, and he continues to serve as well as the Executive Secretary for the Fellowship of Catholic Scholars. In 2000 he was named a Prelate of Honor by His Holiness Pope John Paul II. He is a Knight Commander for the Equestrian Order of the Holy Sepulchre and is a 4th Degree Knight of Columbus.

Endnotes

[1]2 Thess 3:10b.

[2]*New Catholic Encyclopedia*, 1967 ed.

[3]*Ibid.*

[4]*Ibid.*

[5]International Commission on English in the Liturgy, *Documents on the Liturgy 1963-1979: Conciliar, Papal, and Curial Texts,* (Collegeville: The Liturgical Press, 1982), 1443 ff.

[6]Chupungo, Anscar J., ed., Collegeville: The Liturgical Press, 1997.

[7]Jones, Cheslyn, Geoffrey Wainwright, Edward Yarnold, eds., New York: Oxford University Press, 1978.

[8]Henri de Lubac, *Catholicism: Christ and the Common Destiny of Man,* trans. Lancelot C. Sheppard and Sr. Elizabeth Englund, O.C.D. (San Francisco: Ignatius Press, 1988); Louis Bouyer, *Liturgical Piety,* (Notre Dame: University of Notre Dame Press, 1955); Louis Bouyer, *Rite & Man: Natural Sacredness & Christian Liturgy,* trans. M. Joseph Costelloe, S.J. (Notre Dame: University of Notre Dame Press, 1963); Josef Jungman, *The Early Liturgy,* trans. Francis A. Brunner, C.SS.R. (Notre Dame: University of Notre Dame Press, 1959); Karl Rahner, *Spirit in the World,* trans. William Dych, S.J. (New York: Herder and Herder, Inc.).

[9]Francis Cardinal Arinze and others, *Cardinal Reflections: Active Participation and the Liturgy* (Chicago: Hillenbrand Books, 2005).

[10]Patrick W. Carey, ed., *American Catholic Religious Thought: The Shaping of a Theological and Social Tradition,* (Milwaukee: Marquette University Press, 2004), 433.

[11]Megan McKenna, *Rites of Justice,* (Maryknoll: Orbis Books, 1997).

[12]*Ibid.,* 168.

[13]H. J. Schroeder, O.P., trans., *The Canons and Decrees of the Council of Trent,* (Rockford: Tan Books and Publishers, Inc., 1978), 51.

[14]Mary E. Stamps, ed., *To Do Justice and Right Upon the Earth: Papers from the Virgil Michel Symposium on Liturgy and Social Justice,* (Collegeville: The Liturgical Press, 1993), 12.

[15]*Ibid.*

[16]*Ibid.*

[17]*Ibid.*

[18]Mark Searle, *Liturgy and Social Justice,* (Collegeville: The Liturgical Press, 1980), 15-16.

[19]Robert Barron, "The Liturgy as Display of God's Justice," *Antiphon: A Journal for Liturgical Renewal*, vol. 4, no. 3 (1999): 19.

[20]*Ibid.*

[21]*Ibid.,* 21.

[22]Barron, 22.

[23]Mark Searle, ed., *Liturgy and Social Justice,* (Collegeville: The Liturgical Press, 1980), 17-18.

[24]I Cor. 11:17-22.

[25]*Liturgy of the Hours,* vol. 3, p. 182-83.

[26]*The Word Among Us,* June 2006, p. 9.

XII.

Liturgy, Laity, and the Sacramental Sense

Russell Shaw

In this paper I shall examine a state of affairs that antedates *Sacrosanctum Concilium* and the confusions and abuses of the past forty years and reinforces the latter in highly destructive ways. It, too, needs to be part of the reform of the reform, whenever that highly desirable remedial program comes about.

I can best explain what I mean by starting with a story that a friend of mine tells.

Not long ago he took some parents and students from the public high school where he teaches on a trip to Italy. There were twelve or fifteen of them, and they shared the tour bus with others. The trip was a success. Everyone had a dandy time visiting some of the most beautiful places in a beautiful country.

But after a while my friend realized that something funny was going on.

Whenever they pulled into a town square and parked in front of the local cathedral, everyone piled off the bus and immediately started shooting photos of the church. "They began taking pictures before they even *looked* at it," my friend said. "What mattered was shooting those photos. They could *see* the cathedral later, if there was time."

My friend thought that was odd. But I couldn't help thinking that this behavior isn't so different from what happens at a Sunday liturgy in my parish today. The two things may even be related. The emphasis at such a liturgy is on *doing* things, keeping busy, allowing little opportunity to reflect on what's really taking place. *Seeing* things—not just with the physical eyes, but with the eyes of the spirit—gets short shrift. In liturgical celebrations like this, the ideal of full, conscious, active participation that the Second Vatican Council spoke of has been externalized. This is liturgy for people more interested in taking pictures of the cathedral than seeing it.

Some time back I came across a remark by a Church official that inadvertently suggests where this thinking comes from.

> Participation in the liturgy is a common means of
> spiritual formation. Though weekly Mass attendance
> has declined...laity are participating in worship more
> extensively and in greater depth through the ministerial
> roles of reading, singing, distributing communion,
> assisting at the altar, providing hospitality, and so on.[1]

I take this to be a typical statement of a viewpoint that is common today. There are several things to be said about it.

First, the casual dismissal of the decline in Sunday Mass attendance by American Catholics, from two out of three forty years ago to one out of three today, is happy talk.

Second, to equate *doing things*—reading, singing, distributing communion, "providing hospitality," and so on—with full, conscious, and active participation, is seriously confused.

Third, there is absolutely no evidence that this approach involves liturgical participation any deeper and more prayerful than the participation of the largely silent congregations several decades ago. Claims to the contrary are statements of ideology not empirically verified fact.

Fourth, even if one is willing to grant, for the sake of argument, that lay people who *do* these things at Mass are more deeply engaged in liturgical worship than people were fifty years ago, the number of those who *do* them is extremely small, compared with the vastly larger number who do not.

And fifth and finally, what a comment like this mainly expresses is the mindless enthusiasm for lay ministries so common in official circles today. A rational, well-considered concern for full, conscious, and active participation by the laity wouldn't concentrate on the ministries of a few but on the baptismal priesthood, the non-ordained priesthood of the faithful, in which all *Christifideles* participate. As the *Catechism* says: "Through Baptism and Confirmation the priestly people is enabled to celebrate the liturgy."[2] How often these days do you hear homilies saying *that* instead of urging lay people to give Father Bob and Deacon Tom a hand by distributing communion?

But the fundamental problem—the problem of seeing the liturgical celebration with the eyes of the spirit—goes deeper, operates on a very different plane. A lot more is involved than questions of liturgical translations and the structuring of liturgical rites, important as those things are. What we are looking at here is, I believe, the loss of the sacramental sense in Western culture, and it's *that* above all which makes full, conscious, and active participation so difficult. Our immanent, externalized liturgical celebrations simply reinforce this underlying problem.

In modern times, we see a pervasive loss of the sacramental sense and a concurrent hollowing-out of our understanding of what "sacrament" signifies, leaving behind only the shell of symbol. The difference between sacrament and symbol is crucially important. A symbol points to another reality extrinsic to itself; whereas, in the case of a sacrament, the other reality is embodied within the sacramental sign and intrinsic to what the sacrament is and does.

Conventional symbols have a kind of radical arbitrariness: they are subject to being changed. When circumstances dictate setting aside one symbol for something, there is no difficulty about adopting another, as advertisers adopt new logos for products depending on which of their aspects they wish to highlight and which audience they mean to attract.

It is very different with a sacrament. The sacramental sign and the reality it signifies are inseparably joined. Fundamentally alter a sacramental sign, and the reality it signified is no longer there. For example: substitute something else for bread and wine, and you no longer have the Body and Blood of Christ. And, as that suggests, the reality embodied by sacraments is itself unique. Pope John Paul II said:

> What else are the sacraments…if not the action of Christ in the Holy Spirit? When the Church baptizes, it is Christ who baptizes; when the Church absolves, it is Christ who absolves; when the Church celebrates the Eucharist, it is Christ who celebrates it…All the sacraments are an action of Christ, the action of God in Christ.[3]

Where people suppose that sacramental liturgy is only a symbolic act to which those who perform it assign its meaning, the devising of liturgical settings naturally emphasizes values like novelty, ingenuity, relevance, experiment, excitement. Practically speaking, as Cardinal Ratzinger—now, Pope Benedict XVI—has pointed out,[4] they aim to entertain. But the more entertaining the celebrations become, the more support they lend to the belief that what is going on is symbolic, nothing more. By contrast, where it is supposed that the central action is a sacramental act which is primarily Jesus' act rather than ours, the approach will be fundamentally conservative. It will stress values like dignity, gravity, decorum, reverence, devotion, piety, awe. The test of good liturgy will be a test of faith: whether the worshiping community grows in holiness through full, conscious, active participation in the action of Christ.

How did the loss of the sacramental sense happen? There are various accounts. It is suggested, for instance, that the problem began with the fading, somewhere between the Patristic era and the Middle Ages, of a sense of symbolic realism, according to which symbols participate in the reality of what is signified and make it concretely present.[5]

At least three important sources of the problem stand out in modern times.

One is the Reformation and the emergence of the Protestant view of sacrament. Luther believed in the Real Presence, at least in the context of the Eucharistic celebration itself, but his general leaning against sacramentalism is well known. Calvin believed in a "virtual" presence, but over time it was not his view that prevailed among Calvinists but Zwingli's: namely, the view that the Lord's Supper was a purely symbolic rite.

Father Benedict Ashley sums up the implications of the de-sacramentalizing trajectory in Protestantism like this: "For many

Protestant theologians, this de-sacramentalization of Christian life did, and perhaps still does, seem progress toward a more spiritual understanding of the gospel. External rites were replaced by interior experience. But as Luther himself pointed out to those who tried to dissuade him from his belief in the Real Presence, this kind of excessive spiritualism undermines the fundamental Christian belief in the Incarnation."[6]

The second stream in this development is the body-soul dualism identified with Descartes: *Cogito, ergo sum* (I think, therefore I am). Spinoza revised and refined that into *ego sum cogitans*—I, in being conscious, am existent. And so we have a radically dualistic account of the human person, which takes it for granted that the fundamental reality of such a being is mind or spirit; that the body is not very important—indeed, is hardly relevant—in defining the reality of this person; that the external, material world in which bodies live and act has only a kind of attenuated reality and inferior value; and that both things, world and body, may be manipulated to the extent one is able to manipulate them and cares to do that. There is not much room here for incarnationalism and a sacramental sense.

Finally, the critic George Steiner, in his book *Real Presences*, speaks of what he calls the dissolving of the "contract" with language and other media that occurred in literature and the arts between the late nineteenth century and the middle years of the twentieth century. Before then, Steiner says, there was in literature and art, and in those who practiced them and enjoyed them, "a central supposition of 'real presence'": artists and audiences took it for granted that these were signs pointing to a reality beyond themselves.[7]

Steiner attributes the "ontologically crucial first step" away from this central supposition to Stephane Mallarmé. The crucial move by this prominent French poet of the Victorian age was the conscious repudiation of the idea that language refers to a reality beyond itself. Mallarmé was the precursor of a school of poets who held that what really matters about poetry is sound, not sense. At their most extreme, some of these writers strung together nonsense syllables and called them verse.

So, in Steiner's account, we pass rapidly through Nietzsche and Freud, and arrive at deconstructionism, whose lesson is that "where there is no 'face of God' for the semantic marker to turn to, there can be no transcendent or decidable intelligibility. The break with the postulate of the sacred is the break with any stable, potentially ascertainable meaning of meanings."[8] Which, whatever else it signifies, certainly signifies a state of mind according to which any meaning there may be in our sacred gestures—our prayers, our liturgies, our sacramental acts—is meaning *we* place there, not meaning that is simply present as a given. It is pointless to look to prayer, liturgy, and sacraments as thresholds of a realm of transcendence with which they put us in touch.

Ordinary people are not deconstructionists, but *avant-garde* theologians and catechetical and liturgical theorists often more or less are. Through them this kind of thinking has a trickle-down effect on the liturgy. And in this way, too, ordinary people are cut off from crucially important dimensions of sacramental faith.

Where shall we find solutions to our present difficulties? If these difficulties have causes as deep-rooted as they appear to have, that is not easy to say. But as a preliminary attempt at suggesting an answer, here's a story about a songbird and a cell-phone.

As I was attending Mass one morning some months ago, a bird outside the window of the church burst into ecstatic song just at the moment the priest elevated the Host. It was an epiphany that moved me to murmur: "My God, how beautiful that is!" Here was a small intimation of transcendence, an intuition of sacramentality, of the sort that, experienced more intensely and on a larger scale, led the psalmist to sing: "The heavens declare the glory of God" (Psalm 18.1). Or William Blake to write:

> To see a World in a grain of sand,
> And Heaven in a wild flower,
> Hold infinity in the palm of your hand,
> And Eternity in an hour (*Auguries of Innocence*).

A few weeks later, at Mass in the same church, something very different happened. With diabolically precise timing, somebody's cell-phone went off just at the Consecration. My reaction also was different. "[Expletive deleted]," I said to myself.

But later, as I thought about these two incidents, I started to see them in a different light. After all, I asked myself, why shouldn't one find sacramentality and transcendence in the cell-phone as much as in the songbird? The cell-phone is a striking illustration of human communication, and human communication is an image of the divine communication that has its fullest expression in God's self-revelation in and through the Word made flesh. In the cell-phone, too, we see an extraordinary application of human genius that, as Pope John Paul II pointed out, is best understood as a form of co-creation with God.[9] The pope calls the idea of co-creation a central element in a spirituality of work; and we might add that it also is a potential element in recapturing the sense of sacramentality whose loss is at the root of our liturgical woes.

Now, admittedly it is a stretch to imagine someone distracted by a cell-phone during Mass adverting to a papal encyclical in order to be recollected and regain the sacramental sense. Still, the ideas in play here do point to something important. To put it simply: the world can be seen in a sacramental light even now. Here are well-known lines from another poem:

> The world is charged with the grandeur of God.
>> It will flame out, like shining from
>> shook foil;
>> It gathers to a greatness, like the ooze of
>> oil crushed… (*God's Grandeur*).

This of course is the opening of Gerard Manley Hopkins's sonnet *God's Grandeur*, which was written in 1877. It is a magnificent poem, and for our purposes it is interesting in a particular way. The first line—"The world is charged with the grandeur of God"— announces the sense of natural sacramentality that the psalmist and William Blake also expressed. But there is genuine novelty about what follows: for Hopkins affirms that the divine grandeur flashes out "like shining from shook foil/It gathers to a greatness, like the ooze of oil/crushed."

Here is something new. Writing in the same years as Mallarmé, whom George Steiner links to the collapse of transcendence in modern literature and art—Hopkins finds the raw material of sacramentality precisely in the detritus of industrial civilization itself. In this vision, "shining from shook foil" and "the ooze of oil crushed" declare the glory of God.

So, it can be done. The sense of sacramentality remains a possibility. But the question that the example unavoidably raises is this: must one have the same sensibility as Gerard Manley Hopkins in order to have this sacramental sense? If so, most of us are out of luck. And so, too, is any realistic possibility of full, conscious, and active participation in the liturgy, since it absolutely requires the sacramental sense.

In a way, the answer to the question—must we all see with Hopkins's eyes?—is: yes. We *do* need a sensibility like that. But not, thank God, to the same degree or with the same fineness of refinement. We simply need to do the best we can to acquire the habit of contemplation and the way of viewing reality that comes with it. Few of us will be contemplatives of a high order; but if we persevere, by the grace of God we are entitled to have at least modest hopes.

Of course our hope should be realistic. Monsignor Robert Sokolowski calls attention to certain intrinsic limits residing in the fundamental Christian distinction between God and the world: "The world and the sacred have a Christian tone for us because of the Christian distinction in whose light we experience them, and the tone can become more pronounced for those who live the Christian life with greater dedication and love. But such experiencing insists precisely on a unique absence [i.e., the absence of God], on a term that must prompt faith and hope but not direct vision."[10]

This is the voice of philosophy, and in its frame of reference it is correct. But operating within the Christian tradition, we also are entitled to appeal to the voice of contemplation and Christian mysticism.

Philosophy tells us what we can manage on our own. The sense of transcendence in this case is an interpretation of some natural reality—a glorious sunrise, a mighty mountain range. Contemplation also is something like that. But contemplation and mysticism also offer access to a real presence of another sort—a direct apprehension of the presence of the divine which takes place on the initiative of God. At its highest reaches, this experience is shared by very few—a Teresa of Avila, a John of the Cross. But to judge by anecdotal evidence and personal testimony, in its less dramatic forms such direct experience of the presence of God is by no means so very rare.

What does all this have to do with the liturgy? I think it might be put as follows:

The problem of the liturgy today is that for forty years we've been trying to do something that was certain to fail. We tried to have full, conscious, active participation without cultivating the sacramental sense. Our immanent liturgies today are in fact obstacles to doing that. It's like shooting pictures of the cathedral without stopping to see it. Now, if we wish to recapture the art of seeing, we must seek the help not only of philosophers and theologians and liturgists, but especially of poets and saints.

St. John of the Cross speaks of a "renovation" of the spirit which he describes as a direct divine illumination of the human intellect and will, such that the soul becomes "a soul of heaven, heavenly and more divine than human."[11] But this probably is well beyond realistic expectations for most of us. Something more modest and more within our grasp is suggested by the full eight lines of a poem about a common human experience. It is a poem by Emily Dickinson that in its quiet, understated way exemplifies the kind of sacramental seeing I am talking about:

> The bustle in a house
> The morning after death
> Is solemnest of industries
> Enacted upon earth,—
>
> The sweeping up the heart,
> And putting love away
> We shall not want to use again
> Until eternity ("*The Bustle in a House*").

There are libraries full of works by spiritual masters explaining how to practice contemplation. I offer only this advice: The best way to begin is to begin. God does the rest.

Veteran Catholic journalist and writer Russell Shaw is the author of some 17 books, and many, many articles and columns. Notable among his books in addition to the authoritative *Our Sunday Visitor's Encyclopedia of Catholic Doctrine* are such titles (also published by OSV) as *Does Suffering Make Sense?* (1987), *Papal Primacy in the Third Millennium* (2000), *Ministry or Apostolate: What Should the Catholic Laity Be Doing?* (2002), and *Personal Vocation: God Calls Everyone by Name* (2003), this last title co-authored with Germain Grisez. His latest book, co-authored with Father C.J. McCloskey and published by Ignatius Press in 2007, is entitled: *Good News, Bad News: Evangelization, Conversion, and the Crisis of Faith.*

Russell Shaw is a contributing editor of *Our Sunday Visitor* and is also a member of the communications faculty of the University of the Holy Cross in Rome. He was formerly the information director at various times in his career of both of the United States Conference of Catholic Bishops and of the Knights of Columbus. He is a member of Phi Beta Kappa and the Equestrian Order of the Holy Sepulcher of Jerusalem. Married to Carmen, he is the father of five and grandfather of nine.

Endnotes

[1]H. Richard McCord, Jr., "Full, Conscious, and Active Participation: The Laity's Quest," in Anthony J. Cernera, ed., *Vatican II: The Continuing Agenda* (Fairfield, Conn.: Sacred Heart University Press, 1997), 160. Mr. McCord is executive director of the laity office of the U.S. Conference of Catholic Bishops.

[2]*Catechism of the Catholic Church,* n. 1138.

[3]Pope John Paul II, *Crossing the Threshold of Hope* (New York: Alfred A. Knopf, 1994), 130.

[4]Joseph Cardinal Ratzinger with Vittorio Messori, *The Ratzinger Report* (San Francisco: Ignatius Press, 1985), 126.

[5]See Robert Sokolowski, *Eucharistic Presence: A Study in the Theology of Disclosure* (Washington: The Catholic University of America Press, 1994), 198-199.

[6]Benedict Ashley, O.P., *Theologies of the Body: Humanist and Christian* (Braintree, Mass.: The Pope John XXIII Medical-Moral Reseach and Education Center, 1985), 175.

[7]George Steiner, *Real Presences* (Chicago: University of Chicago Press, 1989), 96.

[8]*Ibid.,* 132.

[9]*Laborem Exercens,* n. 25 (1981).

[10]*The God of Faith and Reason* (Washington: The Catholic University of America Press, 1995), 142.

[11]*"The Dark Night,"* in *The Collected Works of St. John of the Cross* (Washington: Institute of Carmelite Studies, 1979), 361.

XIII.

Acceptance Speech for the Reception of the Cardinal Wright Award

Patrick Lee

Thank you!! Thank you very much! I am very, very honored.

Back when I was in grade school, in Dallas Texas—back in the late fifties and early sixties—every year on the Feast of Christ the King, for one day all of us Catholic grade school children virtually took possession of downtown Dallas, or at we did so for a few hours. For on this day, all of the Catholic children who went to Catholic schools, both in Dallas and in Fort Worth—tens of thousands of us— all of us Catholic kids had a formal procession. We prayed the rosary, recited litanies, and sang great hymns, while we processed up and down the main streets of downtown Dallas and then into the large Dallas auditorium, all of us dressed in our school uniforms. There, with the bishop, we celebrated Mass honoring Christ the King.

It is not just nostalgia when I say that that was an experience in which I learned in a concrete way deep truths about Christ and about his invitation to us build up with him and with his grace, his kingdom. These processions helped to drive home to us the truth that because we were Catholics we were different. We were not called to blend into the world, but to work in order to bring all things under Christ's headship. And these processions illustrated the truth that the Catholic faith is something visible and tangible; Christ is active in and through his Church, the body of Christ, carrying on his mission in the world today. And during those wonderful processions, we had a concrete sense that we do have a home, in the Church, and, eventually, in the completed kingdom of God.

The hymn that we sang most frequently on that day was: "To Jesus Christ Our Sovereign King":

> To Jesus Christ, our Sovereign King,
> Who is the world's salvation,
> All praise and homage do we bring,
> And thanks and adoration
> To Thee and to Thy Church, great King,
> We pledge our hearts' oblation,
> Until before Thy throne we sing,
> In endless jubilation.

The Fellowship of Catholic Scholars is in many ways like those processions honoring Christ the king, and in many ways like that great hymn as well. The Fellowship of Catholic Scholars makes concretely present some basic truths about the faith and it gives many Catholics, both young and old, a genuine and fruitful sense of being at home. At these meetings we often see scholars and holy men and women who have indeed, and with fidelity and courage, as the song says, pledged their hearts' oblation to Christ the king. Here one sees and is able to get to know exceptional teachers who bear clear witness to the reasonableness, to the goodness, and to the beauty, of the Catholic faith. And here, one sees a strong and steadfast love and appreciation for the faith, and therefore one might hear in one's ear the distant music of that great hymn, "To Jesus Christ Our Sovereign King."

Faith comes from the Holy Spirit moving us interiorly to accept his offer of friendship and personal communion, which is what revelation is. But there also are external signs of credibility—concrete, visible things about Christ and his Church that show us that our act of faith is reasonable, that it is a morally responsible act, that we ought to do it. These signs of credibility include the holiness of members of the Church, and the sublimity of Christian teaching and of the Church's liturgy. So many dedicated and holy people in the Fellowship of Catholic Scholars—and I think here, for example, of the late Father Ronald Lawler, O.F.M. Cap.—so many have produced, or have been, signs of credibility, paving the way for our act of faith, and showing us that being Catholic is a wonderful gift. Therefore, I am especially honored, and am very grateful, for this award. I am honored and humbled to receive this award from men and women who have such a deep love for—in the words of that hymn—Christ Jesus Victor, Christ Jesus Ruler, Christ Jesus, Lord and Redeemer.

Thank you again. Thank you for this honor.

Patrick Lee is a Professor of Bioethics at the Franciscan University of Steubenville. He is a graduate of the University of Dallas and of Niagara University, and he received his Ph.D. at Marquette University in 1980. Professor Lee's notable book, *Abortion and Unborn Human Life*, was published in 1996. His articles and reviews have appeared in the *American Journal of Jurisprudence, Bioethics, Faith and Philosophy, Philosophy, Review of Metaphysics, International Philosophical Quarterly, American Catholic Philosophical Quarterly*, and other journals. He is the Director of the Bioethics Institute at the Franciscan University of Steubenville, and has recently completed a book, co-authored with Professor Robert P. George of Princeton, entitled *Body-Self Dualism and Contemporary Ethical Issues*

XIV.

Homily of Bishop Finn

**The Most Reverend Robert W. Finn,
Bishop of Kansas City—St. Joseph, Missouri**

Deuteronomy 8:2-3, 14b-16a
John 6: 41-51

Dear friends in Christ, The Diocese of Kansas City-St. Joseph is honored to be host to the 29th Annual Convention of the Fellowship of Catholic Scholars. It is a joy for me to welcome friends from St. Louis, James and Helen Hull Hitchcock, and others at *Adoremus*, as well as this entire distinguished gathering of scholars reflecting on the heritage of the Church in light of the Constitution on the Sacred Liturgy, *Sacrosanctum Concilium*, promulgated by Pope Paul VI at the Second Vatican Council almost 43 years ago.

I am grateful that the address of His Excellency Archbishop Ranjith, of the Sacred Congregation for Divine Worship and the Discipline of the Sacraments, will be read and will establish the framework for our gathering, anchoring us where we wish to be in the maternal heart of the Church. I am confident that the sense of his presence will be renewed and echoed many times through the rich offerings of the presentations of these days.

The place where we are right now was once within the Diocese of St. Joseph, established nearly 140 years ago, and we commend ourselves to his protection as we begin. In the early 1900s the two dioceses of Kansas City and St. Joseph covered fully two thirds of the State of Missouri. Fifty years ago last month, these two great dioceses became one great diocese. This is a Jubilee year for us, and again, I am pleased that it is imprinted with such a gathering as this which honors our Catholic tradition so meaningfully.

The Diocese of Kansas City-St. Joseph is a local Church with a heritage of deep faith. The faithful Catholic community, though comprising about 10% of the total population, contributes much in faith, service, and positive moral influence.

Over this last half-century we have also had our challenges, and in the time since Vatican II, we have been tested, like other places, by misappropriations of the "Spirit of the Council."

Indeed, Kansas City is home to institutions which, on the one hand, have seen in the Council a license to promote the democratization of the Church and to proclaim, in too many instances, a "prophetic freedom" for departing from the most fundamental of Church teachings. On the other side, an international society of clergy and laity that maintain very serious suspicions about the validity of Catholic Church teachings and practice since the Council has established its U.S. base in our Diocese.

The desire we have to fulfill the plan of our Lord Jesus Christ for our unity has been a theme of our Jubilee celebrations, and I welcome the reflections of this Fellowship which I believe will contribute to a more mature hermeneutic on one of its pivotal teachings, *Sacrosanctum Concilium*, and a deeper love for the "sacrament of unity." (SC 26)

In today's first reading, from the votive of the Most Holy Eucharist, Moses bids the people, "Remember! Remember how for forty years now the Lord, your God has directed all your journeying in the desert." Some verses later, he will tell them, "Do not forget! Do not forget the Lord, your God, who brought you out of Egypt, that place of slavery…"

These passages from Deuteronomy are prelude to others calling the Israelites to a conscientious examination of their destiny in God's plan, a faithful acceptance of the covenant, and a canticle of thanksgiving. They are in this way a fitting preamble also to the Eucharistic Liturgy, where the faithful are summoned to remember and give thanks.

The orations and proclamation of the Sacred Scriptures and the preaching of the ordained minister similarly transmit the presence and action of Jesus Christ the living Word, within us and among us. If the *verbs* of the Old Testament – the summons to remember, be faithful, and give thanks—remain the same in the New Testament, the *subjects and objects* of these divinely inspired exhortations are more fully revealed in the New Testament in the person and saving action of Jesus Christ.

Each celebration of the sacred mysteries begins with a call to conversion. The purpose and power of the Penitential Rite is not the same as sacramental Reconciliation, but the ritual has the urgency of the Lord's own Gospel call to repentance, and ends with an acclamation of Christ's Lordship that points to God's mercy.

The worship which we owe the eternal God orients the Church in submission to that mercy, to the adoration of the divine majesty, and to a vision of our heavenly destiny with the suffering souls and the communion of saints.

And can there be true worship without oblation and sacrifice? The one saving sacrifice of Jesus Christ on Calvary, renewed in an unbloody manner on the altar, is the climax of the work, carried out on behalf of the faithful at the hands of the priest, and consummated in a Communion in the Body and Blood of the Lord.

Dear friends, in the Sacred Council the Fathers announced their "desire to impart an ever increasing vigor to the Christian life of the faithful," through "a reform and promotion" of the sacred liturgy (SC 1) which would help it be seen more readily as the very font and summit of the whole Christian life (SC 10). This renewal had everything to do with the dynamic embrace of the acts which are inherent in the mystery of the Sacrifice of the Mass: the remembering, the giving thanks, the interior conversion and change of heart, the adoration due God alone, the oblation of our hearts united to the pierced heart of Jesus sacrificed for our sins, the eating of Christ's Body and Blood in the Communion of the Mystical Body, and the sustaining hope of new life in Christ's triumphant return.

These are the constitutive elements of a "full, active, and conscious participation" (SC 14) which, by the power of the Holy Sacrament itself, is ready to be made alive in the Church and in her members, each time the Lord's sacrifice is offered.

The renewal of the liturgy is mostly about the interior embrace of these various invitations: Repent and change your heart; heed the

Word of the Lord; let the grain fall to the earth and die; take up your Cross; eat, This is My Body; go now and serve the Lord. In the person of Christ the Head, the priest ritually summons us to be joined to the Lord Jesus Christ who has once for all made it possible for us to participate in His work of salvation. The call to renewal in the Second Vatican Council was timely, but it was not a message unique to our age and culture; nor could it ever hope to be accomplished through merely external modifications in vessels, language, logistics, posture, music, art, architecture, or a redistribution of liturgical functions.

This is not to say that any of these latter elements is inconsequential. To the contrary, the Council exhorts holy Mother Church to examine many of these as to their significance in the "restoration of the liturgy." (SC 21, 27ff.).

It is perhaps true that in an earlier era there was a deeper awareness of the transcendent power of the sacred rites and the efficacy and finality of each ritual action of the priest at Mass. In fact, we are celebrating the same Holy Mass, under the same divine mandate, and with the same infallible purpose and result. Certainly we would be at odds with *Sacrosanctum Concilium* and the discipline of the Church if we, as individuals, were to add, remove, or change the well defined elements of the Church's liturgy (SC 22:3).

We would be enriched, as priests, to contemplate more frequently the simple and sublime elements and actions entrusted to us at the altar. We would be more convinced of the awesome reality of their unadorned magnificence, and of who we are as priests and pastors. The faithful would have a less obstructed access to the sacred mysteries which they are meant to have.

At times, it seems as though the pendulum is still swinging somewhere between innovation and restoration, and that we are not much closer to home than when we started. At other moments, it is possible to hope that we are getting near the top of the hill, and some day soon we will fall gently over the tipping point, onto the other side of our disunity and lingering disarray—and wonder happily how we got here and why it took so long. Over the last years the Church's documents, *Dies Domini, Liturgiam Authenticam, Ecclesia de Eucharistia,* the Revised *General Instruction of the Roman Missal,* and *Redemptionis Sacramentum*, to name a few, have given helpful impetus to the continuing reform.

I have prayed much these past months for our Holy Father Pope Benedict XVI, as I imagine him laboring over his anticipated apostolic exhortation, fruit of the synod on the Holy Eucharist. Let us pray for him.

And in the meantime, while in these days we reread and study where we have been and where we must go at the beckoning of *Sacrosanctum Concilium*, we ask for the light and fire of the Holy Spirit. This *Gift* will help us belong completely to the Church with filial trust, and at the same time cry "*Abba*," to the heavenly Father who is wanting to draw us to His Son. "No one can come to me unless the Father who sent me draw him" (Jn 6:44).

We turn to Mary, who adored the Father in spirit and in truth, and was more closely united to Christ's sacrifice than any other human person: O Mother of the Word Incarnate, Mary, Mother of the Eucharist, despise not our petitions, but in your mercy hear and answer us. Amen.

The Most Reverend Robert W. Finn, D.D., Bishop of Kansas City-St. Joseph, ordained a bishop in 2004, automatically succeeded the retiring bishop, the Most Reverend Raymond J. Bolling, D.D., on May 24, 2005. A native Missourian, Bishop Finn was ordained a priest of the Archdiocese of St. Louis on July 7, 1979, after having studied at the St. Louis Preparatory Seminary North, Cardinal Glennon College, and the North American College in Rome. Later, he received a Master's Degree in Educational Administration from St. Louis University. In addition to parish assignments, he has served as a high school administrator, as Director of Continuing Formation of Priests, and as editor of the *Saint Louis Review*, the weekly newspaper of the Archdiocese of St. Louis. He was named a Chaplain to His Holiness in August, 2003, with the title of Monsignor. Bishop Finn is the second in a family of five children, three sisters and a brother.

APPENDIX

FELLOWSHIP OF CATHOLIC SCHOLARS

Membership Information

For information about joining the Fellowship of Catholic Scholars, contact the Executive Secretary, the Rev. Msgr. Stuart Swetland at:

Rev. Msgr. Stuart Swetland, S.T.D.
Executive Secretary, Fellowship of Catholic Scholars
c/o Mt. St. Mary's University
16300 Old Emmitsburg Road
Emmitsburg, MD 21727

TEL: 301-447-3453

E-MAIL: swetland@msmary.edu

For questions regarding: 1) joining the Fellowship; 2) changing your address or biographical information; or the Fellowship Web Page, you may contact:

James Shank
604 E. Armory Avenue
Champaign, Illinois 61820

TEL: 217-255-6625

E-MAIL: james.shank@sjcnc.org

OR: visit the FCS website at:
www.catholicscholars.org

Statement of Purpose

1. We, Catholic scholars in various disciplines, join in fellowship in order to serve Jesus Christ better, by helping one another in our work and by putting our abilities more fully at the service of the Catholic faith.

2. We wish to form a Fellowship of Catholic Scholars who see their intellectual work as expressing the service they owe to God. To Him we give thanks for our Catholic faith and for every opportunity He gives us to serve that faith.
3. We wish to form a Fellowship of Catholic Scholars open to the work of the Holy Spirit within the Church. Thus we wholeheartedly accept and support the renewal of the Church of Christ undertaken by Pope John XXIII, shaped by Vatican Council II, and carried on by succeeding popes.
4. We accept as the rule of our life and thought the entire faith of the Catholic Church. This we see not merely in solemn definitions but in the ordinary teaching of the pope and the bishops in union with him, and also embodied in those modes of worship and ways of Christian life, of the present as of the past, which have been in harmony with the teaching of St. Peter's successors in the See of Rome.
5. The questions raised by contemporary thought must be considered with courage and dealt with in honesty. We will seek to do this, faithful to the truth always guarded in the Church by the Holy Spirit, and sensitive to the needs of the family of faith. We wish to accept a responsibility which a Catholic scholar may not evade: to assist everyone, so far as we are able, to personal assent to the mystery of Christ as made manifest through the lived faith of the Church, His Body, and through the active charity without which faith is dead.
6. To contribute to this sacred work, our Fellowship will strive to:
    *   Come to know and welcome all who share our purpose;
    *   Make known to one another our various competencies and interests;
    *   Share our abilities with one another unstintingly in our efforts directed to our common purpose;
    *   Cooperate in clarifying the challenges which must be met;

- Help one another to evaluate critically the variety of responses which are proposed to these challenges;
- Communicate our suggestions and evaluations to members of the Church who might find them helpful;
- Respond to requests to help the Church in her work of guarding the faith as inviolable and defending it with fidelity;
- Help one another to work through, in scholarly and prayerful fashion and without public dissent, any problem which may arise from magisterial teaching.

7. With the grace of God for which we pray, we hope to assist the whole Church to understand her own identity more clearly, to proclaim the joyous Gospel of Jesus more confidently, and to carry out it redemptive work to all humankind more effectively.

Member Benefits

All members receive four issues annually of the *The Fellowship of Catholic Scholars Quarterly*, which includes scholarly articles, important documentation, book reviews, news, and occasional Fellowship symposia.

All members are invited to attend the annual FCS convention held in various cities where, by custom, the local ordinary greets and typically celebrates Mass for the members of the Fellowship. The typical convention program includes: Daily Mass; Keynote Address; at least six scholarly sessions with speakers who are customarily invited to help develop and illustrate the theme of each convention chosen by the FCS Board of Directors; a Banquet and Reception with Awards; and a membership business meeting and occasional substantive meetings devoted to subjects of current interest in the Church.

Current members receive a copy of the "Proceedings" of each convention, consisting of an attractive volume with the title of the convention theme and containing the texts of the conventions speeches and other material of interest to the membership. Every three or four years all members receive a Membership Directory with current information on Fellowship members (addresses, telephone numbers, faxes, e-mails, etc.).

National Awards

The Fellowship grants the following Awards, usually presented during the annual convention:

The Cardinal Wright Award – Presented annually to a Catholic judged to have done outstanding service for the Church in the tradition of the late Cardinal John J. Wright, former Bishop of Pittsburgh and later Prefect for the Congregation for the Clergy in Rome. The recipients of this Award have been:

1979 – Rev. Msgr. George A. Kelly
1980 – Dr. William E. May
1981 – Dr. James Hitchcock
1982 – Dr. Germain Grisez
1983 – Rev. John Connery, S.J.
1984 – Rev. John A. Hardon, S.J.
1985 – Herbert Ratner, M.D.
1986 – Dr. Joseph P. Scottino
1987 – Rev. Joseph Farraher, & Rev. Joseph Fessio, S.J.
1988 – Rev. John F. Harvey, O.S.F.S.
1989 – Dr. John Finnis
1990 – Rev. Ronald Lawler, O.F.M. Cap.
1991 – Rev. Francis Canavan, S.J.
1992 – Rev. Donald J. Keefe, S.J.
1993 – Dr. Janet E. Smith
1994 – Dr. Jude P. Dougherty
1995 – Rev. Msgr. William B. Smith
1996 – Dr. Ralph McInerny
1997 – Rev. James V. Schall, S.J.
1998 – Rev. Msgr. Michael J. Wrenn &
       Kenneth D. Whitehead

1999 – Dr. Robert P. George
2000 – Dr. Mary Ann Glendon
2001 – Thomas W. Hilgers, M.D.
2002 – Rev. J. Augustine DiNoia, O.P.
2003 – Prof. Elizabeth Fox-Genovese
2004 – Sr. Mary Prudence Allen, R.S.M.
2005 – Prof. Gerard V. Bradley
2006 – Dr. Patrick Lee

The Cardinal O'Boyle Award – This Award is given occasionally to individuals whose actions demonstrate a courage and witness in favor of the Catholic Faith similar to that exhibited by the late Cardinal Patrick A. O'Boyle, Archbishop of Washington, in the face of the pressures of contemporary society which tend to undermine the faith. The recipients of this award have been:

1988 – Rev. John C. Ford, S.J.
1991 – Mother Angelica, P.C.P.A., EWTN
1995 – John and Sheila Kippley,
       Couple to Couple League
1997 – Rep. Henry J. Hyde (R.-IL)
2002 – Senator Rick Santorum (R.-PA)
2003 – Secretary of Housing and Urban Development,
       the Honorable Melquiades R.Martinez (later
       U.S. senator from Florida) and Mrs. Kathryn
       Tindal Martinez
2004 – Rep. Christopher J. Smith (R.-NJ) and
       Marie Smith
2005 – Helen Hull Hitchcock
2006 – Senator Samuel D. Brownback (R.-KS)

The Founder's Award – Given occasionally to individuals with a record of outstanding service in defense of the Catholic faith and in support of the Catholic intellectual life. In 2002, the Award was presented to Fr. Joseph Fessio, S.J., and in 2003, to Fr. Ronald Lawler, O.F.M.Cap.

Presidents of the Fellowship of Catholic Scholars

2004 -	Dean Bernard Dobranski, Ave Maria Law School
2003 – 2004	Prof. Gerard V. Bradley, Notre Dame Law School
2002 – 2003	Dean Bernard Dobranski, Ave Maria Law School
2001 – 2002	Rev. Thomas F. Dailey, O.S.F.S., DeSales University
1995 – 2001	Prof. Gerard V. Bradley, Notre Dame Law School
1991 – 1995	Prof. Ralph McInerny, University of Notre Dame
1989 – 1991	Rev. Kenneth Baker, S.J., Editor, *Homiletic & Pastoral Review*
1987 – 1989	Prof. William E. May, John Paul II Institute on Marriage and the Family
1985 – 1987	Rev. Msgr. George A. Kelly, St. John's University
1983 – 1985	Rev. Earl Weiss, S.J., Loyola University
1981 – 1983	Rev. Msgr. William B. Smith, St. Joseph's Seminary
1979 – 1981	Prof. James Hitchcock, St. Louis University
1977 – 1979	Rev. Ronald Lawler, O.F.M.Cap., Diocese of Pittsburgh